Main

Pest & Predator Control

Pest & Predator Control

Quiller

EDITED BY
Jeffrey Olstead and Glynn Evans

CONTRIBUTORS
Tom Blades, Glynn Evans, James Green, Mathew Manning,
Robin Marshall-Ball, Jeffrey Olstead, Barry Wade

PHOTOGRAPHS
Laurie Campbell, Glynn Evans, Jeffrey Olstead, Nick Ridley
www.RiflePhoto.com

DESIGNED BY
Sarah East, Alistair Kennedy,
Sharyn Troughton.

Copyright © 2011 BASC
First published in the UK in 2011
by Quiller, an imprint of Quiller Publishing Ltd

British Library Cataloguing-in-Publication Data
A catalogue record for this book is available from the British Library

ISBN 978 1 84689 085 7

Printed in China

Quiller

An imprint of Quiller Publishing Ltd
Wykey House, Wykey, Shrewsbury, SY4 1JA
Tel: 01939 261616 Fax: 01939 261606
E-mail: info@quillerbooks.com
Website: www.countrybooksdirect.com

CONTENTS

1 INTRODUCTION

The UK countryside has been shaped by man's demands for generations, and in the past any animal that interfered with man, or his sporting activities, tended to be called vermin. Today we recognise the importance of biodiversity and that, with few exceptions, there is a place for every native species. But when the

balance is upset by a species reaching an unsustainable level or threatening the economic activities of man, legal control may be necessary.

Some pests, such as rabbits, inflict economic damage or destroy habitat, which can indirectly threaten other species. Predators take this one stage further by directly preying on other species.

By that reckoning, of course, the greatest pest and predator of all is man – unless he takes steps to maintain a balance. Nowhere is the natural world free from our influence, and therefore we are under an overwhelming obligation to conserve wildlife and its habitat. This obligation falls especially heavily on those who shoot; in managing land they control the habitat and the wildlife that it supports; as shooters they have the tools to do the job.

That is what this book is about; it sets the framework within which pest control should be exercised and the main methods by which it can be accomplished. It is primarily written to help anyone managing game or wildlife to deal with animals that, in over-abundance, present a threat to game shooting or biodiversity.

Deer are not included, although in some areas muntjac in particular have

become a pest. The complexities of deer management put it beyond the scope of this guide and there are many excellent books already available on deer stalking. You will find them listed in Appendix II.

It is important, from the outset, to realise the distinctions between mammal and bird pests. There is no blanket protection for mammals and those which are not specifically protected may be shot or trapped at any time without the need for further justification. In contrast all wild birds in the UK are protected. However, certain species regarded as pests may be controlled under the terms of general licences. This will be fully explained later but the effect of this is that while pest mammals such as rabbits or rats may be shot for sporting purposes the same does not apply to pest birds.

Grey squirrels are serious predators on song birds.

There is, of course, a sporting aspect to pigeon decoying or roost shooting crows, and this is recognised by government, but this is not a justification for shooting pests and you must understand and comply with the general licences which are explained in Chapter 2.

As well as shooting, other methods of control are also allowed for certain species, such as trapping. Provided you are acting within the constraints of the law you are free to choose which method you employ. This will often be dictated by the animal that you are trying to control and the location. In some areas it may not be safe to use a rifle, and so it might be wiser to trap a pest before humanely dispatching it.

We are fortunate to have this choice, but freedom brings responsibility. In any pest control activity you should always be aware of the image it presents to other people and the importance of public and political acceptability. Ultimately the continued right to all pest and predator control is dependent on each individual complying with the law and best practice.

The need to control pests and predators is undisputed by informed conservationists. It is practised on national nature reserves, by wildlife trusts and by the RSPB. High concentrations of grey squirrels, for instance, can virtually eliminate successful breeding by species such as blackbirds and whitethroat, while grouse moors where pests and predators are controlled typically support 33 different species of birds compared with 15 on unmanaged moorland. The threats to human health from rats, and farm incomes from pigeon are self-evident.

Nevertheless, apart from some alien invasive species, all pests have a role to play in the complex ecosystems of our countryside and the aim of control is to manage, not to exterminate. Sustainability is the watchword.

Carcass disposal

In the Victorian past, gamekeepers sometimes displayed the 'vermin' that they had killed on a gamekeeper's gibbet for all to see, and to impress their employers with their efficiency. Such a public display today could cause a hugely damaging backlash. Yet people are occasionally careless when disposing of the carcasses of pests.

While it is the boast of all good sportsmen – and women – that what we shoot we eat, there are, for most of us, limits. Rabbit and pigeon are delicious, there are plenty of recipes for squirrel and a few backwoodsmen are still happy to tackle rook pie. But few of us would emulate the midshipmen of Nelson's navy for whom a popular delicacy was rat.

Whatever you kill, whether it's for the table or not, must be treated with respect. Never leave carcasses lying around the countryside – they are guaranteed to spark complaints to the local press – and make every effort to retrieve any wounded quarry so that it can be humanely dispatched.

Burial and incineration are generally accepted as suitable ways to dispose of carcasses but the regulations covering the disposal of carcasses are complex and, where wild animals are concerned, have many grey areas. The law can change so for up-to-date-advice you should visit the BASC website www.basc.org.uk

An old-time gamekeeper's gibbet is now unacceptable.

2 THE LAW

It is sometimes frustrating, and in some cases disappointing, that UK law does not allow all pests and predators to be managed easily. In part this is a legacy of short-sighted actions in the past and the lessons of history are clear; where pest and predator control is necessary the right balance must be struck and the law observed.

For the gamekeeper or shooter the UK's wildlife legislation is vast; in England alone there are some 40 pieces of legislation relating to wildlife management and licensing. Therefore there are many pitfalls, and some grey areas, to trap the unwary. As a result prosecutions do occur.

Devolution adds another layer of complexity, with laws varying from country to country within the UK. This book cannot be totally comprehensive and it will only look at the core legislation when considering pest control. It is your responsibility to know the law before you set any trap or snare or shoot at any bird or animal. Ignorance is no excuse.

In law there is a fundamental distinction between the protection afforded to wild birds and mammals:

- all birds are protected unless specifically excluded
- only specifically named mammals are protected

What follows is a brief overview of the key acts and points of the law. In most cases those creatures which can be controlled may only be killed or taken by particular methods and, for some, at particular times. These will be explained in this book when dealing with the individual species. However they are all covered by cruelty laws. These are important in considering humane dispatch but may also cover what would otherwise be legitimate control. For instance, using an air rifle on quarry that it is unlikely to kill but merely wound could give grounds for a prosecution.

CONTROLLING WILD BIRDS

The Wildlife and Countryside Act 1981
The Wildlife and Countryside Act 1981 is a core piece of legislation for the protection of wildlife in Great Britain. It does not extend to Northern Ireland, the Channel Islands or the Isle of Man.

The Act only applies to 'wild animals' including wild birds; these are defined as those that are living wild or were living wild before being captured or killed. It is divided firstly into sections of law and then into schedules that list the animals to which the sections apply. It does not affect game birds which are covered by separate legislation.

The first eight sections of the Act protect wild birds.

Section 1 gives blanket protection to all wild birds. It prohibits the intentional killing, injuring or taking of any wild bird and the taking, damaging or destroying of the nest (while being built or in use) or eggs. It can also prohibit possession of wild birds (dead or alive) or their eggs.

It is through various exceptions to this law, which are defined in the following sections, that we can shoot quarry species and control pests.

So, for instance, we quite legally use Larsen traps, destroy crow's nests and kill or take other wild birds as part of a pest and predator control campaign.

The Act also prohibits the use of certain types of traps and poisons for catching or killing birds and bans the use of bows, automatic weapons, gas, explosives and the use of certain types of decoys.

A final section sets standards for keeping birds in captivity. It states that birds are to be provided with sufficient space to stretch their wings fully, although the general licences allow an exception to some aspects of this section.

General licences

Although all birds are protected, some species may be controlled because they are on what is often called 'the pest list'. This book only looks at the control of the key species of concern to the majority of gamekeepers and shooters.

Many people believe that these 'pest birds' can be killed at any time simply because they are 'pests'. This is not so and ignorance has led to a number of prosecutions. It is essential that you understand the system of general licensing before you tackle pest birds, otherwise you too could find yourself in court.

General licences provide the exemptions that allow us to shoot and trap certain species. When the EU Birds Directive came into force the UK gained a derogation which allows the government to issue licences so that some bird species can be controlled. As a result Natural England in England and the

Magpies raid the nests of game and song birds.

devolved governments in the rest of the UK have to issue licences every year which are approved by Brussels.

This annual renewal allows government bodies (such as Natural England in England) to add or remove species as required. Control methods may also be varied. Changes will always be explained on the BASC website and it is a wise precaution to check, each year, that nothing has altered which could affect your activities.

For each country there are several licences covering a variety of issues including the type of gun you can use and the purposes for which you can control pests. Each one is issued for a specific purpose, such as crop protection, and it lists the birds which may be controlled for that purpose and the methods by which they may be controlled. This may include shooting, use of cage traps, and destroying nests or eggs. Where a licence covers crow, jackdaw, jay, magpie and rook, you can use one of those birds as a decoy in a cage trap for the purposes of the licence.

Most of the birds appear on more than one licence; crows, for instance, may be controlled for both wildlife protection and air safety.

In summary, then, the general licences allow authorised persons to kill the species they list for the specific purposes stated on the licence. The crucially important point here is that last phrase 'for the specific purposes stated on the licence'.

This explains why, in practice, when you set out to control a pest bird you cannot say you are doing it for sport or because the bird is a pest. You must be acting in accordance with one of the licences and using an appropriate method, so make sure you have read them and don't get caught out if challenged. Broadly the licences cover:

- prevention of damage or disease
- preservation of public health or public safety
- conservation of wild birds.

It is a condition of the licences that you must be satisfied that non-lethal methods of resolving the problem are ineffective or impracticable. This is your

personal judgement and there is no obligation on you to have tried non-lethal methods before you shoot.

Under the terms of the general licence an 'authorised person' is the landowner or occupier (or persons authorised by them e.g. gamekeepers) upon their own land or a person having written authority issued by local authorities or a person having written authority issued the relevant statutory authority, regional water boards, river authorities or local fisheries committees.

By definition you do not need to apply for general licences but you are required by law to abide by their terms and conditions. These vary from country to country and between different licences. For example in Scotland you must have read the relevant licence before carrying out any form of control. Elsewhere this is not a requirement, but ignorance of the law is, of course, no defence.

The preventative nature of many licences means that you do not have to actually prove that the bird is doing damage when you shoot it; the fact that it is capable of doing damage is sufficient justification. For instance, magpies through predation can damage wild bird populations and therefore trapping them is a preventative measure to conserve wild birds. Woodpigeons can cause serious damage to crops so shooting them as they come into roost, or whilst you have the opportunity over decoys on stubble, is a preventative measure.

In conclusion it bears repeating that to avoid prosecution you must be specific about your reason for controlling a pest. While it is recognised that there can be a sporting element you cannot give that as a reason for shooting; likewise you cannot just say you are controlling a bird 'because it is a pest'. But provided your primary intention is to comply with the purpose and conditions of the relevant licence you have a legal justification.

You can find copies of all the licences and links to the relevant government information on the BASC website – www.basc.org.uk

Golden rules
- Know the law – licences vary from country to country; read them and make sure you understand them.
- Only shoot for the specific purpose of the licence which covers your activity e.g. crop protection.
- If in doubt, check it out. BASC members can get immediate free advice at the end of a phone.

Specific licences
Occasionally, a problem may arise which cannot be dealt with under a general licence. In this situation a specific licence application could be made, to kill or take a wild bird which is not listed on a general licence, use a method that is prohibited, or allow for the disturbance of certain wild birds.

A good example is where a fishery is suffering heavy predation by cormorants; the owner may apply for a licence to control a certain number of birds.

Class licences
In England from 2011 a series of class licences was launched. Although none

of these directly concerned shooting or gamekeeping activities their development could mark a change in future licensing policy across the UK.

They represent a middle way between personal licences, which you need to apply for and which are judged on a case-by-case basis, and the general licences.

CONTROLLING WILD MAMMALS

The legislative umbrella for wild mammals is far broader than that for birds, but equally complex.

Wildlife and Countryside Act 1981

The Wildlife and Countryside Act prohibits the intentional killing, injuring or taking, the possession and the trade in listed wild animals. It also prohibits certain methods of control for particular species; devices such as self-locking snares, bows or explosive, and the use of live mammals or birds as decoys.

However there are exceptions; for instance animals injured as a result of a lawful activity can be humanely dispatched. That might cover an otherwise protected species that had been hit by a car.

Spring Traps Approval Order (England and Wales) & the Spring Traps Approval (Scotland) Order

It is illegal to use any unapproved spring trap for the purposes of killing or taking animals. These orders list the approved traps, the circumstances in which they can be used and the animals which they may catch.

The stoat is a fearless predator.

All spring traps must be set in natural or artificial tunnels, and certain traps can be set in rabbit burrows. The entrance size to the tunnel must restrict the trap to catching the target species. In Chapter 6 you will find more information on the approved traps and the conditions of their individual use.

The Wildlife and Natural Environment (Scotland) Act 2011

The Bill provides additional regulation for fox and rabbit snare users including the need to use identification tags on snares, record where snares are located and a requirement for all snare users to be trained and accredited.

The Hunting Act 2004 (England and Wales)

This Act prevented the hunting of most wild mammals in England and Wales with hounds. However there are a number of caveats and exemptions. Particular points to note for the gamekeeper or shooter controlling mammalian pests or predators are as follows:

- Up to two dogs can be used to stalk or flush mammals above ground to protect game, livestock, and food for livestock, crops, timber and fisheries. The user must have permission or own the land.
- A single terrier maybe entered below ground provided the user is meeting the terms of the government approved code of practice. The code is available from BASC and can be found at www.basc.org.uk.

The Hunting Act does not prohibit the legitimate use of gundogs.

- It is illegal to use a terrier to dispatch orphaned cubs underground.
- It is illegal for a terrier to hold a fox at bay while a terrier man digs down to dispatch the fox. However a terrier man may dig down to release a terrier stuck underground.
- Using any number of dogs to hunt rabbits or rats is not illegal provided permission has been granted from the landowner.
- Hares cannot be hunted or flushed with more than two dogs. However more than two dogs can be used for the retrieval of shot hares.

The Protection of Wild Mammals (Scotland) Act 2002

In Scotland further protection for wild mammals was brought in two years before England and Wales. In essence the main offence under the Act is the same as that of the Hunting Act. However, there are many complicated exceptions allowing certain types of hunting with a dog which is under control. These include:

- Stalking or flushing targeted wild mammals, for example hares, from cover above ground provided they are then shot.
- Flushing a fox or mink from below ground provided it is shot as soon as possible after it is flushed.
- Retrieving a hare which has been shot, or under specific conditions, using a single dog to dispatch fox cubs below ground and believed to be orphaned.
- Where a dog is being used in connection with the dispatch of a pest species and the intention is to shoot that wild mammal once it emerges from cover or below ground, that person does not commit an offence if the dog kills the mammal in the course of the activity.

These excepted activities are conditional on persons involved being authorised and any killing being as humane as possible.

The Wild Mammals Protection Act 1996

This Act gives protection to wild mammals and makes it an offence for any person to mutilate, kick, beat, nail or otherwise impale, stab, burn, stone, crush, drown, drag or asphyxiate any wild mammal with intent to inflict unnecessary suffering.

Animal Welfare Act 2006

Anyone who is trapping or snaring should be aware that they must comply with the Animal Welfare Act, which places a duty of care on any keeper of animals whether temporary or longer term. This means you have a duty of care to decoy birds and caught birds, or the squirrel you have caught in a cage trap. This act is not concerned with the species or trap you are using. However, culling must be humane and avoid any unnecessary suffering.

SHOTGUNS, RIFLES AND AIRGUNS

The ability to use firearms is arguably more important for the gamekeeper or pest controller than traps and snares. Therefore a through knowledge of the laws governing their ownership, storage, use and purchase is essential.

Firearms legislation is applied to different guns at differing levels of restriction. Standard airguns currently have the lowest level of regulation, followed by standard Section 2 shotguns and, lastly, Section 1 firearms, mostly sporting rifles, are subject to the greatest regulation.

Air rifles with a power output of less than 12ft/lb can currently be owned without the need for a licence. For an air pistol, the power limit is reduced to 6ft/lb. Any airgun with a greater power output is considered a Section 1 firearm. For a standard airgun the only security storage requirement is that you take 'reasonable precautions' to prevent someone under the age of 18 from gaining unauthorised access to it. However, owners are advised to store them securely.

Shotguns are an essential tool in controlling pests and predators. Their versatility and killing power makes them ideal for shooting animals at relatively close ranges.

The law defines a shotgun as a smooth-bored gun with barrels of not less than 24in. Semi-automatic or pump-action

must be restricted to hold no more than two cartridges, with a third in the chamber.

To buy, sell or possess a shotgun you are required to hold a valid shotgun certificate. Shotguns must be stored securely and be inspected by the police. The most popular storage system involves a metal cabinet attached to an internal wall. Shotguns owned by a certificate holder must be listed on the certificate and the police must be informed of each purchase or disposal.

Rimfire rifles, centrefire rifles, high-powered airguns and some shotguns require a Section 1 firearms certificate. This certificate specifies the exact calibre, number and type of guns and outlines the purposes for which each may be used. Initially a firearms certificate limits the use of the rifles to land which is specified or approved by the police.

More experienced firearms certificate holders may be granted a certificate with no limiting conditions, usually referred to as an 'open certificate'; this allows the certificate holder to use his/her rifles anywhere he/she judges it to be safe and appropriate, within the law. Security for Section 1 firearms is similar to that for shotguns except ammunition is required to be locked away securely (ideally separately). The amount of ammunition for each rifle is also listed on the licence.

Further information is available on the BASC website www.basc.org.uk BASC members can call the dedicated firearms team on 01244 573010.

All the advice given in this book is, as far as we can tell, accurate at the time of going to press. But laws are constantly being reviewed and it is crucial that you keep abreast of developments. You will find most of what you need to know on the BASC website www.basc.org.uk or contained in the codes of practice issued by BASC.

If you are a member of the association you can get free personal advice by calling or emailing the relevant department. Contact details are in Appendix 2.

3 SHOOTING FOXES:
ambush, high seat, lamping, driving

The general rule that shotguns are for shooting close-moving targets and rifles for longer range static ones holds true for foxes.

Both shotguns and rifles are suitable for fox control, although it is important to be aware of their limitations and those of the person using them.

Shotguns can be used at close range; research by BASC suggests that at ranges up to 30 metres (33 yards) a 12 bore loaded with 36 grams of No.1 or No.3 shot is very effective.

Most rifle calibres are capable of killing foxes humanely in the right circumstances. For the serious fox shooter a centrefire rifle will be the weapon of choice, but if you asked ten different fox shooters which is the best calibre you would get ten different answers. Common calibres include the centrefire .22s such as the .222 or .22-250. Some people will opt for something larger. The .243 Win is a popular calibre for those who want one rifle suitable for foxes and deer.

You must, of course, have foxes included in the conditions on your firearms certificate and some, although not all, police forces tend to be unhelpful if you wish to use a larger calibre. It is the person pulling the trigger and not the calibre of gun that is safe or dangerous. Remember, if you pull the trigger it is you who has the responsibility of making sure it is safe to do so.

Shooting from a high seat; this rifle is fitted with night vision.

The principal methods of shooting foxes with a rifle are either by ambush in daylight or searching for the foxes with a lamp at night. Since foxes are largely nocturnal, lamping is usually the better alternative, but shooting from a high seat or suitable spot at dawn or dusk can be very effective.

AMBUSH

Foxes tend to be creatures of habit so if you know a fox is taking a certain route you may be able to intercept it. You can also, to some extent, predict

the likely routes that foxes will take. They will usually take the easiest choice if it is safe to do so. An undisturbed fox that has used the same path without disturbance will continue to do so until disturbed.

Given the fox's acute senses and your restricted vision a ground-level ambush is likely to be less productive than shooting from a high seat, with a commanding view of a likely area. This has the advantage of a wide field of vision, often provides a safer shot because of the downward angle and there is less chance of being detected by the fox. By measuring the distance to nearby objects such as trees, you will be able to judge the distance of a fox more easily.

For a succesful ambush you will need to be well camouflaged, and in a comfortable position because a long wait may be involved. In selecting your spot remember to ensure that there is a good backstop and that you are downwind of the fox's chosen route.

Another way of using high seats to good effect is to attract the fox to you by using baits and lures. Foxes, being opportunists, will often recognise any easy food source. A particularly effective bait is a pigeon plucked roughly – tear off some of the meat with the feathers and spread these around the area that the fox has been seen in. Not many can resist stopping and examining feathers left in this manner and this can give you the chance to take a shot.

Foxes also recognise smells and sound so these can be used most effectively. A simple rabbit squealer made from a piece of hazel stick, some old cassette tape and electrical insulating tape are all that is required to produce a cheap but highly successful fox call.

Good camouflage is important when ambushing foxes.

The type of squeaky child's toy that you squeeze can be good, or you can opt for one of the more sophisticated electronic calls. While these are expensive they have the advantage of being adaptable and you can tailor the sound to the time of year and prey or attraction that will be most effective. For example, the call of a vixen in the breeding season can be a better attraction for a dog fox than an easy meal. These calls can also be put to good use lamping.

One point of caution with using a call is that the fox will be looking for the source of the sound so it is important to be well hidden, although there are some calls with a speaker that work remotely at some distance from the shooter, attracting the fox to the target area. Finally, avoid calls that are specifically designed for varmint shooters in the United States as these can be considerably different.

LAMPING

One of the most effective ways to control foxes with a gun is by shooting at night – lamping. This involves patrolling an area, usually in a vehicle or ATV, or sometimes on foot depending on conditions, scanning the landscape with a high-powered lamp and catching the fox in the beam so that it can be shot. This is usually done with a rifle, though a shotgun with a suitable cartridge could be used at close range.

This method of control demands absolute discipline and an almost obsessive regard for safety. Above all you must be certain that you have correctly identified your quarry. Simply seeing a pair of eyes shining in the light isn't enough. You must be certain without doubt that it is a fox. You must be equally certain of an effective backstop. There have been very few accidents involving lamping, but they do tend to be fatal.

Knowing the lie of the land

The first priority is always safety. Before lamping always thoroughly check in daylight the land you are going to shoot. Familiarise yourself with it and look for any obvious signs of activity. Make sure that you know where safe shots can be taken and more importantly where it would be advisable not to take a shot. Do not, however, ever assume that because there was nothing in a field earlier that it is still empty; there could be livestock or other hazards in there now.

Do not go lamping unless you are adequately insured.

The equipment

Pages could be written on equipment, calibre and type of rifle, type of scope and so on. Again it is down to personal choice.

With regards to the rifle itself, will it just be for foxing? If you are going to travel round in a vehicle then a heavy rifle, often called a varmint rifle, is a good choice as it is easier to hold steady and designed to shoot small targets at long distances. But should you plan to walk any distance this extra weight can soon become apparent and a lightweight stalking rifle might be a better choice. Deciding on the most suitable rifle will often involve a degree of compromise.

Sound moderators, once a rarity, have become almost uniform on foxing rifles. There are many benefits, especially through reduced disturbance.

As to choice of scope, the options are endless; buy the best quality you can afford. The reticle is an important consideration; heavy cross hairs and posts, while good for stalking at close range in low light, are a poor choice for longer-range work on fox-sized targets. Thin cross hairs are popular. Common sizes of scope are 6x42 and 8x56; variable power scopes are much improved from the past but are considerably more expensive. In general a better quality fixed power rather than a cheaper variable will be the best choice.

There are also specialist night vision scopes which are becoming increasingly popular for the dedicated fox shooter. As with most equipment it is important to research different products and usually you get what you pay for. Good night vision is always more expensive than comparable conventional scopes and is limited to night use, although there are some convertible day/night scopes. Always try before you buy.

A good quality reliable lamp is crucial, and it's often worth having a spare as when they go wrong it is always at the most inconvenient time or place!

Power is a matter of personal choice: many people favour a high-power lamp of 800,000 candle power or higher. This makes it easier to identify a fox if you are going to use a filter that dims the intensity of the beam. A set of coloured lenses is worth investing in, particularly for use on lamp-shy foxes. Red is generally the most popular. However, some people prefer to use a less powerful lamp so as not spook the fox.

Once you have identified a fox it is always wise to keep it on the edge of the beam, rather than in the centre, to minimise the glare.

If you are using a vehicle you can simply plug in the lamp but if you are going on foot a separate power pack will be needed. Technological developments have made these considerably lighter than in the past, but make sure you get one with sufficient power for your lamp.

There are many other items that you might carry with you or in your vehicle and these should include:

- Your firearms certificate (remember it must give authority for both the intended quarry and area of land.)
- Written permission.
- A first aid kit.
- Torch, which can be useful for locating a shot fox.
- Mobile phone (on silent).
- Hot drinks and some food if you are out a long time.

The list can be almost endless but the important thing is to make sure that you are safe and comfortable at all times.

Setting out

Having done your homework, and being fully familiar with the ground in daylight, there are some other essential preliminaries.

Speak to who ever has given you permission; let them know when you are planning to go out and ask if there are particular places that a fox is working or areas that they wish to be left quiet. Tell them when you expect to start and finish. Tell them how many people will be involved and what vehicles are being used. Make sure that anyone who might need to check who is out, has your contact details and that you have theirs in your mobile phone.

There is no legal obligation to give the same information to the local police although this can sometimes be wise, depending on location. If you do tell the police, ask for the log entry number. This can save unnecessary problems if they are called out to investigate by a member of the public.

Reporting back

After you have been out, report back to the landowner or keeper all activity and sightings of note and let them know if you were successful. They will appreciate this information and it demonstrates to them that you are reliable and conscientious. If you are going out alone it is very wise to have a procedure in place to let someone know when you are finished and home safely.

When to go

The darker the night the better and ideally there should be enough wind to muffle the noise and carry your scent away from the quarry, although a great many foxes are taken on nights other than this. Foggy or very wet nights are definitely unsuitable, although after or before heavy rain can be good.

The best time of year is often just as the harvest is reaped when well-grown cubs are making an appearance and becoming more adventurous – before they have become wise in the ways of the world. Lamping, however, is a year-round activity and you should always be familiar with what is going on in your patch.

Shooting foxes in the late winter and early spring will have the maximum benefit for livestock and wildlife by reducing the potential breeding population. But that isn't the end of the job – foxes will readily and quickly re-inhabit ground when previous incumbents have been dispatched.

Although foxes are active in all the hours of darkness it is a good idea to vary the times you go; some of the most successful periods for lamping are early in the evening and the last couple of hours of darkness, but any time can be productive.

Lamping is essentially a team effort. Although it is possible to lamp on your own, working as a team is often more effective. On foot this will generally mean that one person operates the lamp while the other shoots. Using a vehicle, such as a pick-up, a team of three works well, one to drive and two on the back (with a suitable frame), one lamping and the other shooting. Each member of the team should know exactly what they are going to do under every circumstance.

With a good team, there should be little need to talk, since each person knows their role inside out. Safety is paramount because with safety you will have confidence and with confidence comes success.

Tactics on the ground

On a lamping night keep the routine simple. Begin by lamping into likely or favoured areas. Once the perimeter has been covered, move into the ground. Try to work into the wind; this hides both scent and noise from your quarry. Often, though, when using a fox call, a fox will approach from downwind. There's no need to panic, these foxes are usually running keen and will frequently present a shot.

In areas where there has been a lot of lamping you will often find foxes become lamp-shy. Obviously this is when night vision equipment can prove its worth, but there are other tactics to overcome the problem. Try a different route or time, try a filter on the lamp or change to a different colour.

When you have a fox in the beam remember not to rush shots and always correctly identify the target; just because you have seen a fox in an area do not assume that a pair of eyes in the same spot is the fox. Never shoot until you are one hundred per cent certain.

The waiting game

In an area where you know a fox is working it is possible to mount an ambush instead of going out lamping. Around dusk or dawn, when no illumination is needed, you can quietly wait in a favoured spot and use a call or bait to attract the fox. If you know the likely direction of approach you can make sure that you are well concealed and that there is a reliable backstop. Experience will teach you the best method of use relevant to your area and circumstances.

It is worth remembering that if a fox has been called in with a rabbit squealer and missed, the sound may subsequently have the opposite effect – rather than being an attraction it might actually alarm the animal.

If you are successful always try to retrieve your kill and dispose of it appropriately either by incineration or deep burying. If you are unable to find it at night, or if you think you may have wounded a fox, make all possible efforts during the following daylight hours to find it, or tell the landowner or keeper where a dead animal may be.

Remember that as responsible shooters we have moral and legal obligations that we must observe.

To sum things up:

- Always take the time to get the basics right, and then continually practise.
- Be familiar and competent with the chosen rifle.
- Learn to judge ranges under all light and weather conditions.
- Always be absolutely one hundred per cent sure to identify the target correctly.
- Always check for a safe backstop before squeezing the trigger.
- Never take a chancy shot in the hope of hitting the target; only shoot when you are confident of your abilities.

If you do use a vehicle, it is essential to stay on the farm lanes and fields and not be tempted to shoot from a vehicle (or on foot) from one of the many public country lanes surrounding the land. In most cases this is illegal and could cost you your certificate. Make yourself familiar with the BASC Lamping Code of Practice and Section 19 of the Firearms Act 1968, and the Highways Act 1980, Section 161 in England and Wales.

Rabbit squealer

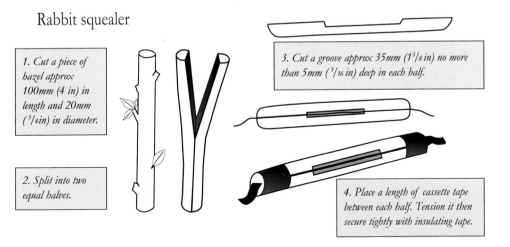

1. Cut a piece of hazel approx 100mm (4 in) in length and 20mm ($^3/4$in) in diameter.

2. Split into two equal halves.

3. Cut a groove approx 35mm ($1^3/8$in) no more than 5mm ($^3/16$in) deep in each half.

4. Place a length of cassette tape between each half. Tension it then secure tightly with insulating tape.

The key to this little gadget is not to blow too hard, otherwise you just sound like a rabbit that has been feeding on curry, and the cassette tape will tear under its tension. Do not have too large a mouthpiece, an effective seal is important. Experiment and make several squeakers to get the right sound. Some will be a waste of time, but others will be dynamite. It is not unknown to have several foxes coming at the same time and approaching to within a few yards.

FOX DRIVING

Different types of fox control vary in their efficiency, and fox driving would probably not be at the top of most people's list but there are times when driving can give excellent results, where other methods will not. There are places where lamping and snaring are impractical because of livestock or public access so driving an area may be the best method of control.

Fox drives can be held at any time of year. In the spring you may be trying to get to grips with a vixen before she has cubs. Later in the year you may turn your attention to release woods; although this may not result in foxes being taken it can give you some peace of mind prior to release.

The best time for a fox drive is when you know that a fox is in the area; this sounds rather flippant but if a fox has been going quietly into a wood in the morning there is a good chance that it is planning to lie up there during the day; this would be an ideal opportunity for an impromptu drive. You should also keep your eyes open to spot any new earths and if you are walking through the woods the smell of fox is hard to miss.

The use of dogs is usually considered unwise and must not contravene the Hunting Act, although sometimes, depending on where you live in the UK, hounds may be used for driving foxes to the gun. In many places there are gun packs as well as formal hunts and these are often called upon by gamekeepers to clear the woods before poults are put into release pens. If you have a gun pack or other hunt in you vicinity you can liaise with them. They will organise the event, brief the participants and generally run the show, but in general this is only necessary where there are large woods and a number of foxes.

The average shoot will seldom need to call in the cavalry, particularly where it is responding to an immediate threat. Organising a drive is relatively straightforward. However, as with all shooting of ground game, it is important to be properly organised and everyone should be briefed.

When you are planning the shoot it is a wise precaution to inform anyone in the area who might be affected, such as horse owners. If there is public access ensure that walkers are unlikely to stray into the wood during the shoot and that they are not disturbed by numbers of camouflaged people waiting on the woodland's edge with guns.

Before the shoot a detailed briefing is essential. All participants must be told what they can and can't do or shoot. They must know how the Guns will be set out and what signals will be given to start and end the drive.

Basically you have two lines of Guns; one walks while one stands. The walking Guns are essentially operating as beaters, though a fox may often break back through the line or try to sneak out at the side. Standing Guns are placed strategically around the wood to drop the fox as it breaks cover. If driving a large area there may be quite large distances between Guns, especially on the flanks, and distances can vary. The topography will usually dictate the best places to stand Guns, but corners should always be covered.

Although the layout of the wood may influence the direction in which it is driven, the general rule is that you should drive downwind. That will help to move the foxes in the direction you want them to go – towards the standing Guns, which they will not scent.

The standing Guns will take up their stations either being dropped off by vehicle or walking into position; at this stage it is essential to be quiet; no talking is the general rule. Guns must be unobtrusive, so wear clothes that blend in with the background, paying particular attention to hands and face; a pair of lightweight camouflage gloves and a net mask will help with concealment.

This, however, creates a problem. If you are invisible to the fox it's a fair bet that you're invisible to other Guns as well. It's impossible to over-stress the importance of knowing where other Guns are and, in the interests of self-preservation, making sure they know where you are.

When in position familiarise yourself with your location; usually you will stand close to the woodland edge to be less obtrusive. Foxes will often come to the edge quietly and look before breaking cover.

Try to get in a position where you have the most time to spot a fox, especially before it is alarmed, and you can take your shot while it is still or moving slowly.

Get yourself comfortable, check your arc of fire, and then it is a case of standing still, not moving, and waiting. Do not shoot at anything other than foxes unless you have been told to do so, which is most unlikely. If a fox approaches but is not in range, do not shout to warn a neighbouring Gun: if he is paying attention – and he should be – he will have seen it.

Only shoot at a fox that is in range for your gun and ability; it is well worth patterning your gun beforehand with the cartridges that you plan to use. There is much talk as to which size is best, but BASC has carried out extensive research using a wide variety of guns and loads. The conclusion of this is that the limit for any shotgun to ensure a clean kill is 30 yards (27m). Before the drive begins it is worth pacing out 30 yards (27m) to a landmark which will help you judge range when a fox appears.

As already mentioned, the minimum recommended load is 36 grams but if your gun is capable of taking a heavier load, by all means use it.

If a fox comes your way do not move or raise your gun until just before you fire; if you hit the fox do not be afraid to give it a quick second barrel to make absolutely sure.

Finally, always stay in position till after the drive, even if you have had a shot. Moving out of position may confuse neighbouring Guns or put you in danger, so stay where you are until the signal for the end of the drive is given.

For a walking or driving Gun the rules are similar; you too will line out quietly, this is most important especially on a short drive with the wind blowing towards the standing Guns because noise carries.

Although the need for concealment is less important for walking Guns they may well be ploughing through brambles and undergrowth, so make sure you're

Foxes will steal the eggs of ground-nesting birds.

wearing something tough and thornproof, but with plenty of ventilation because it can be warm work.

When the signal is given by the person in charge, the walking Guns set off in line. It is crucially important to keep the line straight. If you are in front, or lagging, you may make it impossible for a neighbouring Gun to shoot a fox that breaks cover, and at worst you may end up getting shot yourself.

Always be aware of your neighbours and don't be afraid to give a warning if one is pushing too far ahead, or call for the line to pause if one needs to catch up. You may be strolling down a ride while another Gun is struggling through a briar patch or over fallen timber, so don't hurry the drive; you can, however, make plenty of noise to push the fox forward.

Usually you can fire at any legitimate quarry that is in range provided you know where the standing Guns are. Generally all forward shooting will cease when you are getting close, but this should have been covered in the pre-shoot briefing.

4 FOX BOLTING WITH TERRIERS

The Hunting Act 2004 prohibits all hunting of wild mammals with dogs in England and Wales, except where it is carried out in accordance with one of the tightly drawn exemptions. These allow for certain necessary pest control, subject to strict conditions. As a result of representation from BASC the use of terriers to bolt foxes to protect game was included in the exemptions.

The government accepts that on shoots it is necessary to ensure that serious damage to game birds or wild birds is minimised but it recommends that you should consider the full range of options before deciding to use a dog underground.

You can find details of these options in Natural England's species information note *The Red Fox in Rural England* which can be downloaded at: www.naturalengland.communisis.com

It is a legal requirement that the dog is used in accordance with the code of practice (*see* Appendix I). BASC has also drawn up a good practice guide; this has no legal force but sets out a sensible framework for working terriers and if you stick to it you will be very unlikely to run into legal problems. You can download it from the BASC website.

Failure to comply with the conditions of the exemption, or with the code, will mean that the use of a dog below ground to hunt wild mammals is no longer exempt hunting. It will therefore be a criminal offence that may result in prosecution and a fine of up to £5,000.

We all know that terriers include a wide variety of dog types but, for the purpose of this code, terrier actually means any type of dog used underground to bolt a fox. And bolt is all it can do; the objective is to flush the fox to standing Guns. Nets can be used to constrain the fox on bolting and can often aid the process of the fox being shot in a controlled manner.

Putting theory into practice

There has been a lot of confusion about this law and it has led to keepers and landowners resorting to trying other methods to protect their birds. But terriers are still a valuable tool in game management provided you stick to the rules. And – most importantly – you stick to foxes. With the growing number of badgers in the UK, and strict laws protecting them, you must be very careful about entering a terrier to bolt a fox. One hole can look like any other, so it's important to distinguish an earth which a fox uses from a badger sett.

The first factor is that foxes will mainly go to ground when it is cold and they will use a number of different earths scattered across the countryside. Badgers stay in one place; they live in a sett which usually consists of several holes in one place, and use them day in, day out. This means the wear at the mouth of the tunnels is much greater and there are normally ample signs of occupation.

Badgers move huge amounts of soil, fox earths rarely show much disturbed soil, and if you look more closely you may come across small, dug-out scrapes which will be full of badger excrement; fresh

Fox print   **Badger print**

bedding pushed out at hole openings to air in the daylight is common too.

Foxes, on the other hand, have an unforgettable, pungent smell – the earth often reeks of fox. They can also leave pad prints at the earth openings and it is not unusual to see feathers and remains lying around, particularly in the springtime when vixens will be taking food back for their cubs. Another good indication is fresh fox scats.

Badger sett showing signs of wear and large amounts of soil.

Fox earth smaller with much less disturbance.

What you will need

The law says that you need written permission from the landowner, stating you are operating in accordance with the exemption from the Hunting Act to protect game birds and wild birds on the land stated. This permission must be the first thing which goes into your pack and you must always carry it with you when you are performing terrier work below ground, and produced it if questioned.

Locator with collar.

Secondly, the law states that dogs which are entered below ground must wear a locator collar, then, if the dog becomes stuck, you can locate it and dig down to rescue it. This is the second thing to go into your pack.

Thirdly, you should consider taking fox purse nets. These are very handy in areas where it is not safe to discharge a shotgun; they can be used to restrain the fox for immediate humane dispatch.

Finally you need to carry a torch and spade. A torch in case you run out of daylight and need to find the way back to the car – or, in the event of an emergency, it could signal an SOS. It also makes it easier to look into tunnels if a dog gets stuck. The spade is vital if the dog needs to be rescued.

Armed with the necessary equipment you now need to know how to work within the exemptions to the Hunting Act.

Bolting to the gun

It is usually too much for one person to enter the terrier and shoot as well, so make sure you have a competent Gun with you – preferably someone who has done it before and knows the drill.

It is also important that you think it through, assess the ground where the fox is bolting and ask the question – is it safe?

The Gun must know at all times where the person entering the dog is, and, of course, know the dog. You don't want to risk losing your terrier if it emerges from the earth close on the fox's heels.

Entering the terrier

Having first confirmed that the earth has been used by a fox, you must take all reasonable steps to prevent risk of injury to the dog and you must comply with the code of practice for England and Wales issued by the Secretary of State:

- The terrier's role is to locate and flush the mammal, not to fight with it.
- Only 'soft' terriers which stand back and bark are to be used.
- Care must be taken to ensure the safety of those involved and to minimise the risk of injury to either the terrier or the wild mammal.
- The terrier's time below ground must be kept as short as is possible.
- The terrier must always be fitted with an electronic locator.
- Once it is determined that a terrier is trapped, assistance must be given to release it immediately

In Scotland the legislation covering hunting was introduced by the Scottish Parliament and is slightly different. The rules for terrier work are broadly similar and you must ensure that:

- Reasonable steps are taken to ensure that the fox (or mink) is flushed as soon as reasonably possible after it is located and is shot as soon as possible after it is flushed.
- Reasonable steps are taken to prevent injury to the dog, including steps to prevent the dog becoming trapped underground and, if it does become trapped underground, steps to ensure it is rescued as soon as is possible.

- The person is in possession of a firearm for which they hold a valid firearm or shotgun certificate.
- The person is the owner or lawful occupier of the land on which the activity takes place, or is acting on behalf of them and with their permission.

The Act also permits (subject to the above requirements), the use of a dog below ground in order to locate a fox cub(s) which you reasonably believe is orphaned. But only if you take reasonable steps to ensure that, once located, the cub is dispatched by a single dog, or otherwise killed as humanely as possible.

Remember that the law is absolutely explicit on the kind of terrier you can use. It states that no dog should be entered if it is known to be 'hard', i.e. if it's known to fight or kill underground. Only dogs that bay up and show enough presence to bolt the fox should be entered.

This inevitably presents an unpleasant truth. Controlling foxes in the springtime – when it can be most effective and necessary – you may come across a vixen with cubs. In England and Wales if the cubs remain underground they must be left to die; it would be illegal for you to allow your dog to kill them underground. Accidents can, of course, happen, but the onus is on you to show that you had no intention of breaking the law. In Scotland, as explained previously, this is not a problem.

Occasionally there is more than one fox at home, so the Gun, after dispatching a fox, should always be prepared for a second shot. Only when the dog has exited can you give the Gun the nod to put his shotgun in the slip ready to move on to the next earth.

Foxes are adaptable animals and recognised earths are not the only places you can expect to find them. Field drains are often used for temporary shelter and where they are long, and at times dry, they can be fox havens. As long as there is a clear exit for the fox to bolt it is perfectly legal to enter your terrier.

The most important thing to remember with this exemption from the Hunting Act is that the welfare of the fox and the terrier is paramount. When this is jeopardised in any way you should not proceed; by persevering you could not only compromise the good reputation of shooting and gamekeeping but also end up breaking the law.

5 FOX SNARING

Although snares have been used since time immemorial today's fox snares are anything but old-fashioned. They have constantly evolved and there is a continual movement to improve designs and methods to make them even more humane and efficient.

Prior to the Wildlife and Countryside Act 1981 snares could be killing devices with locking mechanisms that continually tightened. Now, by law, they must be free-running and they are, quite rightly, nothing more than restraining devices designed to catch and hold the fox without injury.

As with much advice in this book, the starting point must be to understand and comply with the law. Over the past 30 years snares have come under considerable scrutiny and legislation is different in the various home countries; it is vitally important to understand and comply with the rules.

It is your responsibility, as the person setting the snare, to ensure that it complies with the relevant law. Do not rely on the word of the shop assistant, manufacturer or even the headkeeper that your snares are legal for your country.

The BASC website with its advice and links is a good place to start, while the *Snaring Practitioner's Guide Scotland*, and the Defra Code of Practice give guidance on the minimum legal requirements and on best practice.

HOW SNARES WORK

The snare works because the fox is unaware of its presence, so, when set correctly, it will be capable of taking foxes that have become wary of other methods, such as those that are lamp-shy. The snare can also be used where other methods are impractical, for instance where it would be unsafe to use a rifle.

At its most basic a snare is similar to a simple dog lead – made with a thin but strong wire cable. The aim is to get the fox's head inside the loop before he realises and to restrain him, and that requires a considerable amount of skill.

Although good snares will have incorporated different design features they are essentially variations on a common theme and it is important to view all these features as a whole. They are all interdependent and coupled with the correct methods of setting the snare will ensure that it is efficient and humane.

The cable must be strong yet light; some people prefer a stiffer wire which loops and sets easily; others a softer, more flexible wire, but in general a compromise of sufficient strength and flexibility is often best.

The snare is fastened by crimps, these need to be sufficiently strong to prevent breakages that result in an animal escaping or, worse still, breaking free with the snare attached to it. A refinement, presently under development, is to incorporate a weak link that is strong enough to hold a fox but will break before any other crimp, allowing a larger animal to break free.

The running eye – in whatever design – must be free running. Swivels are fitted to prevent the snare becoming kinked, unravelled or over-wound and thereby risking breakage.

The stop is a small crimp on the wire which prevents the snare closing beyond a certain point. This is a legal requirement in Scotland but not England (an example of why it is essential to understand the different laws) although a stop is always advisable. The accepted minimum distance, at present, for the stop to be fitted from the eye is 23cm (9in). This feature helps prevent injury to non-target species; should, for instance, a deer catch its foot in the snare it will not close beyond a certain point and will simply fall off. Smaller animals can pass through it.

The snare has to be fixed in position; this is usually by a special fastener supplied with some snares, or a loop and shackle. Both have advocates; the first allows precise adjustment of the length of snare but can, if not correctly attached, risk slipping. The loop and shackle will not slip and are easy to change and replace but make it less easy to adjust the length of the snare.

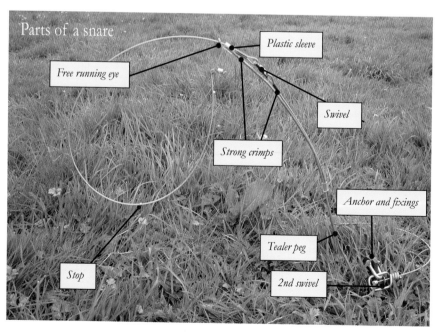

Parts of a snare

Plastic sleeve

Free running eye

Swivel

Strong crimps

Anchor and fixings

Tealer peg

Stop

2nd swivel

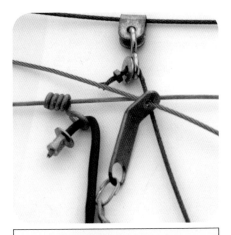

Shackle used to attach snare to anchor.

Running eyes come in various forms.

An anchor will be needed; this must not only be secure enough to hold a fox but also any non-target animal that may be caught. There are various designs and all can be well suited to different locations. Angle iron cut to a length of 450mm x 25mm (approx 18 x 1in) will suit many conditions. A hole drilled 50mm (2in) from the top and fitted with a shackle is a good fixing point for the snare. A stake puller, however, is often needed to remove the anchor from the ground after use. A clever innovation being marketed by some suppliers is a spiral rod that simply unscrews when you want to move it.

Bullet ground anchor.

Spiral rod used as anchor should be hammered flush to the ground.

Another means of securing is the bullet or Iowa ground anchor – a piece of stout metal rod which is knocked into the ground with a special bar. Attached to the middle of the rod is a length of snare wire and loop, which when pulled, as the name implies, turns it into an anchor. Another innovation of this is the addition of an extra length of wire and loop; this is fitted to the end of the anchor and not the middle and, when pulled, instead of setting the rod as an anchor it releases it, so it can be used and moved again.

Whatever anchor method is used it should be as flush to the ground as possible, to prevent the snare winding around it. Posts and saplings, which could also cause entanglement, should not be used. The modern snare has been designed to minimise injury to both foxes and non-target species. In the past snares may have been fixed to drag poles, but this is now illegal in parts of the UK and frowned upon in others, again because of the risk of entanglement.

Preparation

To some degree all new snares will have a manufacturing smell and some have a residue of oil to prevent rusting on them, while many manufacturers coat the wire to prevent rusting. This is a potential problem since foxes have keen senses of smell and sight and the whole purpose of a snare is to avoid detection until it is too late.

However, there is a simple way to rid snares of this newness – boil them.

Use an old boiler or large pan, add a small handful of washing soda crystals to lift the lubricant, and boil for about an hour. Then make sure you remove the surface film from the water before you extract the snares – otherwise all your good work will have been wasted. Having skimmed-off the surface film you can put a mixture of bark chip, leaves and suchlike in the water to dull the colour of the wire.

However, many keepers prefer to avoid boiling by simply hanging the new snares outside so that they become naturally weathered. Whatever you do, the important thing is to check that the snares still move easily and are free-running.

The more snares you run, the greater your chance of catching foxes, but you also increase the risk of catching non-target species. Therefore it is important to choose the location and times that you snare carefully.

Avoid areas that could cause problems – runs near badger setts, areas with brown hares, fields with livestock, public footpaths and near houses where there is a risk of catching domestic animals. There is a long list and every area has its own need for assessment.

Target areas of known fox activity and learn to spot the signs of foxes; paw prints, the strong musty fox smell, long red hairs caught on bushes and fences, droppings and signs of fox kills. Learn also to recognise the signs of regular activity by non-target species and if you are in any doubt do not set a snare.

Sometimes experience will tell you that a fox is about without the obvious indicators, but avoid setting snares just in case a fox comes by. It is much more effective to set them when they will give maximum benefit; when, for instance, wild birds are nesting or when the height of cover makes lamping difficult.

Setting the snare

The first thing you need to determine is where to set the snare – and that involves identifying the run that foxes use regularly. Although these can be

A fox will usually choose a dry, easy route and that is where to set the snare.

anywhere, remember that foxes will usually take the easiest path; this could be along tractor wheelings in a field or a path in woodland.

It is best to set snares in places where the fox will be travelling at a steady pace, so avoid obstacles and places where it may slow down, such as the edge of the wood. If you are snaring on a wheeling in crops, always set a few metres into the field where the fox will have started moving at an even pace. It will then tend to carry its head at a constant level so you have a better chance of estimating the correct height to set the snare.

In woodlands, rides can be bushed-up with thin twigs (remember to avoid the risk of entanglement) to encourage a fox to take a route through a snaring gap. However, a much better idea is to leave a section of cover long when you are cutting rides. Then cut or tread a narrow path through it and set on here. But don't spoil a natural path by trying to bush it up – if you set your snare properly you definitely do not need to this.

Having picked the spot you can put the anchor in and attach the snare.

Hazel pegs, which are easily available, are widely used as tealers or pricker pegs for holding the snare in place. Depending on the location you may use one or two pegs.

Hazel fits in well with the natural woodland surroundings, and although some people say that it will hold the human scent this does not seem to be a common problem. A thin wire rod can also be used and is both effective and discreet.

There are different views on setting the snare; some people will use a snare on a long tealer and allow it to hang down with the running eye at roughly 11 o'clock; others prefer to set it from the side at roughly 9 o'clock. The important thing is to make the snare and peg as unobtrusive as possible.

Many people have a rigid idea of the size of the snare and of

Tealer pegs made from wire and hazel.

the height at which it is to be set. The codes of practice recommend a minimum height of 20cm (8in) to the bottom of the snare loop, but remember this is a minimum and not a rigid rule.

The old keepers' advice was that the shape of your hand laid flat with your thumb up was roughly the size of a fox's head and that the height to your thumb tip from wrist was the right height for the snare bottom. However a height of 23–25cm (9–10in) and loop in the region of 18cm (7in) works very well and this can reduce the risk of catching badgers.

The snare's length should be as short as possible to minimise movement and avoid the injury of any animal caught.

Snare in woodland run.

Snare in wheeling.

When running snares always walk the path that the snares are on; never walk round them or foxes will do the same, and try to keep the path as close to fox width as possible. When setting and checking snares stand or crouch in the run to avoid broadening it. If it does become too wide you can bush it up but always keep this to a minimum and keep things as natural as possible; if there are dried plant stalks nearby use these.

Finally, always avoid strong and unnatural smells on your hands, clothing and footwear.

Advanced snaring

It is possible to snare in gaps in hedges and fences but great care must be taken when doing anything which risks injuring a fox or other species. Quite large animals will push through narrow gaps in fences and hedges, and if this is a possibility an alternative method must be found. A technique to minimise the risk of a fox being injured is to have two anchor pegs, one near the obstacle and one away, with a running wire between them. The snare is set to this wire via a one-way lock mechanism running away from the obstacle; thus when a fox is caught it travels away from the risk of entanglement.

The technique often referred to as a midden or 'fox grave' can be particularly useful if there are deer, livestock or other non-target species on your ground which make conventional snaring on runs difficult. The idea is to fence off a piece of ground (preferably thick with rushes, bracken or briar) to keep out the livestock and make some runs within it that are baited and snared.

You can put up a secondary fence around the bait, leave holes in it and snare the holes. Always use a small-gauge wire of sufficient height and snares of a short length to prevent anything caught either jumping over or becoming injured.

The bait, either food or a scented lure, can be used in the area before the snares are set, or the midden may be run in the winter when food is scarce. Always remember to comply with legislation regarding animal by-products and be aware of the public sensibilities with regards to middens; any food bait should be buried and not left on the top.

If using a scent lure, a good tip is to place it slightly off the ground on something like a tree stump as this helps the wind carry the scent. There are commercially available scents but some people have their own recipes, usually based on animal fat from the Sunday roast with a little salt and fish oil mixed in.

What to do when you have a catch

A captured fox should be killed swiftly and humanely, ideally with a shot to the head. If it is moving about in the snare then a shot to the heart area followed by a head shot may be appropriate. Insensibility and death can be checked by touching the eye, perhaps for safety's sake with a stick, to test for blink reflex.

Replace and reset the snare as appropriate and dispose of the body responsibly; deep burial would be suitable.

When checking your snares, apart from a gun there is some other equipment you should have. You will need tools and materials to replace damaged snares and anchors. A pair of good quality wire cutters is a must and if you are not carrying a garden or muck fork you should have easy access to one. If you catch something capable of biting you, that must be released, you will definitely wish you had carried one with you. A hessian sack or a jacket will be useful when releasing non-targets (see below).

Despite following all the best practice guidance you may sometimes catch non-target species. Unless the animal is badly injured and has to be killed on humane grounds, it must be released immediately. If it has to be dispatched, then use the same humane method as for killing a fox. Remember you may be called upon to justify your action in court.

Releasing non-target animals from snares can be difficult. The animal's struggles should be limited. Take the fork and walk to the snare's anchor point. Put the fork tines over the wire and run them out along the wire close to the animal's head. Then push the fork into the ground (without using your foot, to avoid the risk of being bitten). This pins the animal by the neck. A blunt hook slipped under the wire enables it to be raised from the neck and then to be snipped with the wire cutters. Covering the animal's head with a hessian sack or your jacket to restrict its vision can often calm it. Always cut the snare at the noose in order to ensure that no part of the snare remains on the animal. Never cut the snare anywhere else in the hope that the noose will fall off later.

6 TRAPPING SMALL GROUND PREDATORS

Tunnel traps have long been a mainstay for controlling small mammalian predators such as stoats and rats; used properly they are humane and extremely effective. But first make sure that you are familiar with the law and the type of trap needed for the species you intend to catch.

The laws on trapping are very specific – you can only use traps that are legally approved and they can only be used for the species for which they have government approval. They are listed on the Spring Trap Approval Order, and you can find details of this in Appendix I.

This means, for instance, that one of the most commonly used traps, the Fenn Mark 4, can be used for grey squirrels but not for rabbits. So setting one in a rabbit burrow would be illegal. The larger Fenn Mark 6, however, can take all the species listed for a Mark 4 plus mink and rabbit. So before you buy or set a trap, check with the Approval Order to make sure you get the one that is legal for the species you are targeting.

The law doesn't just cover the types of trap but also dictates how they may be used. All spring traps must be set inside a natural or artificial tunnel, which is, in each case, suitable for the purpose. This does include a rabbit burrow if the trap is approved for rabbits. It is an offence to set any spring trap in the open or to use approved traps in unapproved circumstances, which may result in prosecution.

In a recent court case, a pest controller used a Fenn Mark 4 to catch a mink, stating as his defence that mink came within the definition of 'other small ground vermin'. The judge disagreed, found him guilty of using a trap to catch an animal it was not approved for and imposed a £600 fine plus costs.

Traps should be inspected at least once every day. It is of the utmost importance to fully understand and comply with the law and any relevant codes of practice, especially since the law can be different in each of the home countries.

Drainage pipes in a dry spell are good places to set a trap.

Equipment

Once you know the law you can progress to actually setting some traps. At its most basic, all you need is:

- the traps
- material to build the tunnels
- a means of fixing them in place.

In practice you will need a more few items of equipment, none of which need be overly expensive.

Firstly there are the different types of trap and all can be useful in the right circumstances. Imbra and Jubys (although no longer made) are excellent for catching rabbits in burrows. For tunnel trapping probably the most commonly used would be a Fenn Mark 4, these are relatively cheap to buy and if looked after will last many years. They fit nicely into a tunnel and their design is such that when they go off they actually jump slightly and 'grab' their target to ensure a swift dispatch.

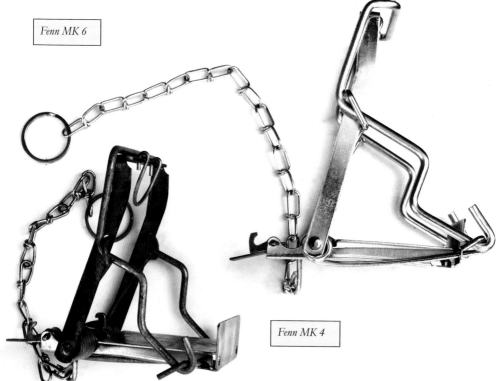

Fenn MK 6

Fenn MK 4

Legal traps

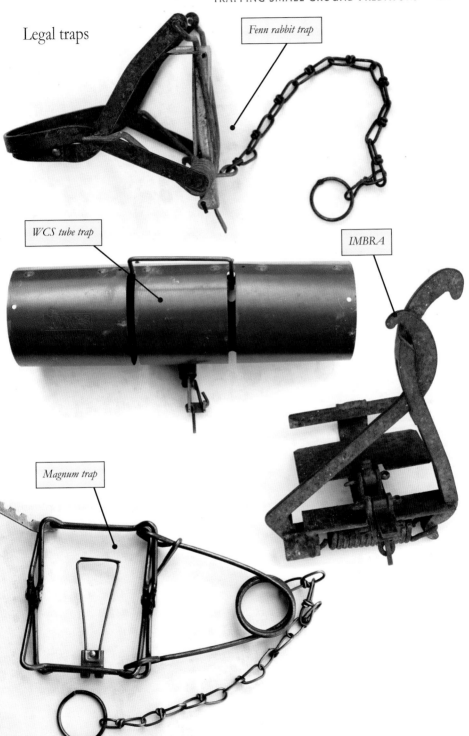

Fenn rabbit trap

WCS tube trap

IMBRA

Magnum trap

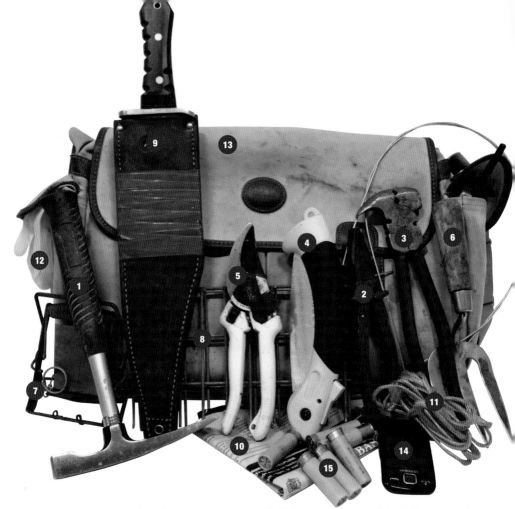

Let's now consider the equipment needed for trapping and building tunnels. Firstly a spade: this need not be expensive but the shape and size are important; either a rabbiting or border garden spade is needed. They are just the right size for cleaning in the tunnel and can also move reasonable amounts of earth. Avoid folding or large garden spades as they are not suitable for this job.

One of the most important items is a proper trapping hammer (1); years ago you could buy these as such, today a genuine one is something of a rarity and the best solution is to buy what is generally called a brick hammer. One end is for knocking in nails, but the other end has a flat blade which is ideal for cutting through turf and roots when setting the trap.

Then you need pliers (2) – general purpose or fencing pliers (3). They too are multipurpose and can be used for cutting and tying wire, adjusting traps, removing staples and so forth.

A folding saw (4) and a pair of secateurs (5) are very useful for cutting and trimming pegs to anchor traps in place; they are also handy to achieve a neat finish.

A hand fork (6) is also useful, especially to break up the soil round the tunnel and to keep it fresh. Although the hammer can be used for this, the fork is a useful refinement; it also frees you from carrying a spade on a daily basis.

A spare trap (7) and homemade folding tunnel (8) should, if not carried, be easily available for those opportune chances to catch predators. The tunnel pictured is made out of weld mesh and is designed to fold neatly in the bag. It is ready to be used as and when a temporary tunnel is needed.

A means of trimming grasses and weeds is essential for maintaining the tunnels when the cover is growing. A large knife (9) does these tasks; one with a blade of 23cm (9in) or more may look excessive but it is really useful and its sheer size means it has replaced the need for a separate billhook and grass hook. A plastic bag (10) is useful for carrying carcasses and baler twine (11) is always handy.

You might also carry rubber gloves (12) to protect you from diseases that pests such as rats can carry. In fact you should always wear gloves when handling rats.

All this equipment will need to be carried, so a good comfortable bag (13) with a wide strap that spreads the weight evenly and does not dig in is essential. The ideal bag will also have extra pockets for putting different things in such as radios, mobile phones (14) and cartridges (15).

You'll also find the bag is handy in the summer when you do not want to wear a jacket and, at all times of the year, it can be used to kneel on when the ground is wet, or to protect your knees from thorns.

Finally, it is important to remember to keep the bag and all equipment away from strong scents such as diesel and creosote, which can contaminate them.

While a 4x4 or ATV will help you to get around the shoot there may well be places that you can only reach on foot, and obviously you don't want to carry unnecessary items or be constantly walking back to the vehicle for tools. So make sure your bag is well organised, plan what you'll need – check that you've got it before leaving the vehicle – and try not to carry something that is overly heavy and you seldom need.

Planning

Building tunnels and setting traps is the easy part; the difficulty comes with checking them every day. When planning to set a round or circuit of traps, try to have your route planned so that you do not spend time back-tracking where you have already been. If you have only an hour or two available each day, walk the circuit you plan before setting the traps to make sure that it's feasible. A good site may be identified, but consider whether it is worthwhile if it takes you many extra minutes to check. And remember to allow extra time for eventualities.

Before embarking on a trapping campaign it is worth deciding what you are setting out to achieve. Are you trying to encourage wild stock, protect newly released birds or perhaps combine the two? Is there a particular species that is presenting a problem? Is there a risk of catching the species you are actually trying to protect? This might happen, for instance, if you are attempting to control mink and water voles wandered into the trap.

You may also need to change your trapping strategy with the seasons. A circuit giving a good, even spread in the spring might be reduced and the traps moved to locations around release pens in the summer to give added protection.

It is in the spring when game birds and other ground nesters are sitting on their nests that they are most vulnerable. Running traps before and during this period will give them the best chance of rearing chicks to adulthood. However, since small mammals do not travel great distances it is worth keeping your traps running throughout the year and because a trap is on duty 24 hours a day it is always protecting wildlife, even when you are not on the shoot. But do not be tempted to run traps when you cannot check them, even if they are regularly catching.

Finally, an often overlooked benefit of working a circuit of tunnel traps and snares is that it gets you out on the ground, covering the shoot. Since all traps and snares must be checked daily, you will see what's going on and others will see you on patrol. This may act as a deterrent to those people with less than honourable intentions, but do remember to vary the routine and the direction in which you go round.

Preparing the trap for use

All new traps will have a residue of 'factory' smell. There is often talk of the need to bury them for a while but this is a fallacy; hanging the traps outdoors to weather is all that is needed. If you are in a hurry they can be put into service straightaway from the shop but, as with all pest control, planning ahead is always wise.

Adjusting the plate – too low.

Often new traps, or even old ones, will need adjusting. The trigger plate should be just in the right position: not too high or too low. It is easy to adjust. If it is too high, cut a strong peg, place under the plate and bend downwards. If it is too low, push upwards to the desired level.

Adjusting the plate – too high.

Just right.

As well as preparing new traps for use it is sensible to maintain older ones. It's best to pick the traps up for the summer when you are not only busy rearing birds but the cover and crops are high and traps at their least effective (traps work best when predators are channelled into a small area).

When you lift the traps, pull the chain not the trap; if you simply yank on the trap itself to free the peg you may well damage it. They are a very strong, simple design but the chain fixing is designed to hold the trap in place from a fox or suchlike carrying it off, not to withstand you heaving on it. If you pull the trap your extra strength can detach the two.

Location

Suitable sites for tunnel traps.

It is all well and good knowing the law, planning the route and deciding what you are trying to catch but the key to success, apart from the trap itself, is the location and build of the tunnel itself.

The key to this is to think of woods as reservoirs for pests and hedges as the pathways that connect them. It follows, then, that the points where the hedges meet the woods should be protected by a tunnel trap. On open land each hedgerow should have a tunnel at either end to provide protection and, in woods, cross rides should be covered.

Gateways are another effective site for a trap. These represent danger to predators that do not like to be caught out in the open, so an inviting tunnel is particularly attractive, before or after making the dash across.

Logs or planks across bridges can give excellent results and a useful tip is to have them slightly at an angle.

Anywhere that is inviting to these predators – a potential food source (such as a release pen) or any interesting place for them to explore will all produce results. Try, when building a tunnel, to have as many of these features as practicable in mind and incorporated in your design.

The tunnel itself can be built from pretty much any material. Often you will read and hear the advice to use a tunnel made from slabs of wood (remember that over time they can close in, so a wooden bar to keep them spread the right distance is a good idea). These are effective but there are often better materials to use.

The basics of the tunnel are that it should, as much as is practicable, fit into its surroundings. At the end of a hedge, or in a gateway, a tunnel made from brick and tiles, suitably covered in turf, is sturdy and has a natural feel. The same tunnel construction would look out of place in a wood where a pile of logs will be more in keeping.

Often the best materials are the easiest ones to obtain. If there is stone in the hedges, then use this; there is little to be gained by making wooden boxes when the best natural material is to hand. If you can find a supply of plastic pipes of the right size, or ones that can be easily adapted, they make great tunnels and have the added benefit that animals such as moles do not interfere with your trapping.

Identify trapping sites

Natural holes in trees or drainage pipes in a dry spell are good and relatively easy places to set a trap. A little cleaning out soon produces a suitable tunnel and remember that a tunnel does not need to have two entrances to be attractive and work well. All that's required is that it blends in and appears natural in its surroundings.

Natural hole...   *...with trap set.*

Good trapping sites are by gates and hedgerows.

The first example site has been chosen after considering the following factors. It is on the side of a small stream where mink have been suspected, so a larger trap (Mark 6) is to be used. There are no water voles so a spring trap is a sensible option. It is on the corner of the wood with the stream and hedge channelling pests along the bank. There is also plenty of natural material in the form of logs near by to build and dress a tunnel. The second example site is along a new hedge line in a gateway. Since this is away from sites where a mink would be expected a Mark 4 trap will be used.

Prepare the trapping site

Having found the right site, dig the tunnel area out and break the soil up (pictured below); any roots that interfere with the build and future setting will need to be removed. Remember that the actual run through should normally be level with the ground. It is often necessary to dig down in order for the finished tunnel to blend in.

Building the tunnel

The first tunnel is to be made using just the logs that are to hand; it is a good idea to measure the actual tunnel hole and make it fit the specific type and size of trap you will use. The second tunnel is to be made from brick. Putting the bricks big side down with one on top of the other makes a good tunnel and doing it this way makes it very strong and stable.

Measure the width of the tunnel.

Bricks should be used big side down.

Rather like building a stone wall there is a correct place for all the available logs and it is just a case of fitting them (above left). The brick-built trap (above right) should be made the correct length and the top of the tunnel should be covered in soil prior to turf (below left).

You will often find that the inexperienced trapper will build a tunnel from wood, uncovered and not fitted into its surrounding. It will work to some extent but a little extra effort will pay dividends; always make a trap look as natural as possible.

Cut a turf a suitable distance from the tunnel, place on top (above right) and tap into position with the back of your spade. Any overhanging turf can be trimmed off. The trap should not only look natural but actually seem inviting.

You can build up the bank to either side of the tunnel entrance or use natural features so that animals are funnelled towards it.

With the finished tunnel with trap in place, securely stapled to the large post, fix the trap with a staple or a large metal or wooden peg (below left). This will prevent a fox or similar from carrying off anything you have caught. Two stout pegs front and rear, leaning inwards, help prevent larger non-targets from entering but also guide pests over the plate and into the centre of the trap, thus aiding a humane kill.

Finished, the trap itself bedded in and lightly covered with soil is, to all intents and purposes, invisible. When correctly set it should ensure a humane kill, which is the aim of all trappers.

Brick hammer and peg.

Sticks narrow the tunnel entrance.

Setting the traps

There is much spoken about setting traps; often you will hear talk of the need to wear gloves so that you leave no smell; this is nonsense, although you must not allow strong unnatural smells to contaminate the trap site. Gloves, however, are a sensible precaution against diseases, especially when handling rats.

Having spent time and effort building a tunnel properly, novices often spoil their chances by not setting the trap correctly. Taking a Fenn as an example, it is designed to jump when it is sprung and catch the animal in its 'jaws' from the side, ensuring instant dispatch. Always set it with the jaws parallel to the side of the tunnel so it works this way.

The first step is to make a small, level indentation in the tunnel the size of

trap, pushing the soil to both sides of the scrape. Bed the trap in so it will be flush with the ground and does not move (above left).

Smooth the soil out on both sides of the trap so it is level and press it down. There is some difference of opinion as to whether it is best to cover the trap or not; if it is a wet area where the soil is sticky it might be wise not to, but in the normal course of things always cover with soil (above right). This covering soil should be run through the hands and fingers so it is small and crumbly, free from stones and other objects that can interfere with it working properly. Once set it should be invisible. Lastly do not forget to take the safety catch off.

A lead of 'fluffed' up soil similar to what you might see outside a rabbit burrow is recommended: this will attract and guide pests into the tunnel, it will improve success rates and is always recommended. However in areas where interference with traps is a possibility you may wish to be a little more discreet. When arranging these lead-ins always mark three lines, one either side and one at the end and work between these. The hand fork is ideal for this, remember to 'work' and move the soil towards as well as away from the trap as over time, if you only go one way, you will end up with dips and holes.

Advanced trapping

A series of tunnels around the shoot will catch a significant number of small ground predators. There are, however, other little techniques that can be used at different times. Earlier you will have seen mention of a portable tunnel carried in the 'trapping bag' with a spare trap. This can be most useful when an opportune moment presents itself whilst patrolling the shoot. You may find a hole that has a pest resident, or find what is often known as a 'stoated' rabbit.

A kill made by a stoat is unmistakable; there is a bite to the back of the neck, usually with a little flesh eaten. Often, having made a kill, a stoat will return to feed later.

Having found the victim – in this case a rabbit – it is important to recognise the different and distinct signs that will indicate which predator has killed it. If you are uncertain you should not set a trap.

In the picture (above) the wound to the back of the neck has all the signs of a stoat. Decide – as with all trapping – if the location is suitable. For instance, is it away from paths or a farmyard where cats or birds may be scavenging? Having decided the site is acceptable you can begin to set your trap.

Firstly place the rabbit in a suitable position, ideally under a little cover of a hedge where it can't be seen by scavenging birds. Secure the rabbit with pegs made from sticks cut from the hedge – stoats are strong and might easily drag the carcass away if it isn't pegged down. If you have to move the rabbit a short way, into a better position, it does not usually matter.

Trim the grass where the trap is to be set – a pocket knife is ideal for this; keep the grass as it will be needed later.

Make a small indentation and set your trap, so it is flush with the ground and steady; make sure it is firmly anchored in place, just as you would in a tunnel. In the illustration below a Fenn-type trap is used but you could use another approved trap just as easily. With the grass you cut earlier, and more as necessary, cover the trap. It is important to cover the trap fully; use your knife and cut the grass into small pieces, this prevents large tufts from clogging the trap and preventing it working efficiently.

Use the portable tunnel to cover the trap, making sure this, too, is firmly anchored in place and fully covers the trap; also remember to restrict the entrance with two pegs.

Make a surround of cover, so as to guide the stoat into the tunnel and cover and camouflage the tunnel.

You will usually catch the stoat reasonably soon after setting the trap and if you have not caught it within a couple of days it is unlikely that you will be successful. Do not keep a trap running longer than necessary and remember, as with all traps, to check it at least once a day. It is often the case with this type of trapping that you can catch one stoat and reset the trap to catch another, especially when stoats are hunting in a group. The more frequently you check it the more likely multiple catches are.

A similar technique can be used to run baited traps. This works best in the winter months when there is no risk of fly eggs and maggots to spoil the bait.

One of the best baits would be a rabbit cut in half and pegged down at the back of the trap, but other baits can be used according to the target species. Maize works well for squirrels, although you would be surprised at the number which come to a meat bait, and in the spring an egg placed at the back of a single entry can be good for stoats and rats.

Where there is a rat problem you can get good results by trapping along established runs. By law, tunnels must cover the traps; wire is usually best but it should be stout and the entrances should be narrowed. Otherwise set them as you would in a portable tunnel, fully covering the trap.

Bridge trap set in place.

Rats are clever animals and soon learn to avoid the traps and tunnels, so only keep them in place for a couple of days; you can replace them again after a break of a few days.

The bridge trap (opposite) is simply a trap set on a plank or pole where pests cross water or other obstacle. If you are using a Fenn trap it is a good idea to measure and cut a step so the trap sits flush when set. You might put soil on the trap to hide it, but this is one of the rare times when it may not be necessary to do so, provided the trap is set as described.

7 TRAPPING MINK:
live catch and tunnel trapping

A ll the trapping techniques previously described will be effective for trapping mink, but be aware that you must use the correct size of trap in order to comply with the law.

You must also remember that mink are often present where other protected species may be found. Accidentally killing a water vole, which has full legal protection, would defeat one of the principal reasons for trapping mink, which have reduced the water vole to being one of our most endangered species.

But mink predation is by no means limited to voles. The first time you begin to suspect a mink is present is usually when moorhens and coots go missing, and you may find that many of your mallard broods fail.

Once the mink has cleared the riverside of its wildlife it will move inland because, unlike the otter, it is not water-dependent and merely uses watercourses as a hunting corridor. When mink move onto dry farmland woe betide any ground-nesting birds – skylarks, lapwings, partridge and pheasants will all be easy prey, and while it is a reasonably straightforward matter to fox-proof a pheasant pen, protecting your birds against a mink attack is much more of a problem.

Tunnel traps can provide some measure of protection around pens, but it is usually better to control mink along watercourses before they move onto drier ground. However, if protected species are also occupying the riverbank, tunnels and Fenn traps should not be used.

LIVE-CATCH TRAPPING

The only answer is to use a live-catch cage trap. The obvious advantage of this type of trap is that any non-target species that are captured can be released unharmed.

Basic kit

Live-catch cage traps come in all sizes and mink traps are mid-sized in the range. Make sure the one you choose is made of sturdy mesh and the trap door shuts securely. Also check that the release rod can be set fine so that the pressure plate is sensitive to the lightest touch. Finally, see that the cage has an external carrying handle so it can be picked up without your hand coming within biting distance of an angry mink.

To secure the trap, and prevent it moving with an agitated animal inside, you can fix several long tent pegs around the sides of the trap, or a long metal spike can be pushed through the mesh and into the ground underneath. Whichever method you use, make sure the pegs do not interfere with the operation of the trap door, and that the cage, cannot be moved.

Another essential part of the kit is pair of thick leather gloves. Non-target species may not realise that you are trying to set them free and will peck, bite, or kick their handler. You will also need to handle dead mink, and sometimes rats, to remove then from the cage, and gloves are essential for this.

Don't forget that water margins are a favourite haunt of rats and wearing gloves gives some measure of protection against Weil's disease. To back this up you can also carry a pack of antiseptic wipes in your car and give your hands a thorough going-over after visiting the traps.

Finally, you will need a suitable gun to dispatch the captive animal. Rimfire rifles pose too much of a threat in ricochets and although an air pistol may seem convenient, it is seldom powerful enough to do the job, even at point-blank range. So, to achieve a humane and instantaneous kill, use an air rifle. Any gun in good condition generating upwards of 8ft/lb will perform quite adequately. A shotgun can be used but you should stand well back from the trap – at least 10 yards – to avoid ricochet or serious damage to the trap.

If you are using an air rifle, two plywood combs are useful so that the animal can be confined in a small space in the trap for shooting.

Trap placement

The techniques described for constructing tunnel traps also apply to the siting of live-catch cage traps, but in addition there are many places where traps can be placed 'above ground' with every chance of success. Mink use waterways as hunting corridors and the likelihood of successful trapping can be increased with a bit of careful observation and planning. It's time to start scrambling quietly round the bankside vegetation!

Bankside trap locations.

Once you have selected a site for the trap, make sure it is pegged down securely and concealed with vegetation or other natural material. Mink are very curious animals and will search out all manner of nooks and crannies in their quest for prey, so the entrance to the cage must look mysterious and inviting to a hunting mink.

As with all live-catch traps, the law requires you to check it at least once each day. If you can only manage a single daily visit, try to make it in the morning. Mink are active at night and to leave one trapped in a cage all day is not good on ethical or humane grounds. Twice-daily visits should be made whenever possible – the second as late as you can manage so that non-target species can be released promptly.

When you cannot make daily checks, close the door of the trap and leave it in 'safe mode' until you have time to resume trapping. Twice-daily, or even daily visits to your trap demand a commitment that few people can make for any extended period, but don't despair, there is a solution – the mink raft.

Mink rafts

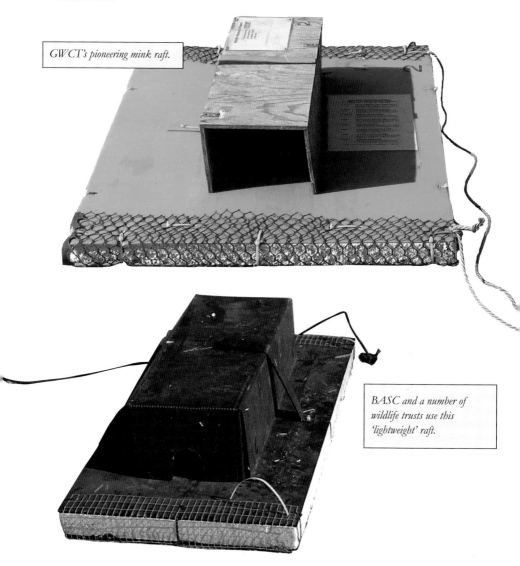

GWCT's pioneering mink raft.

BASC and a number of wildlife trusts use this 'lightweight' raft.

Although rafts have been used for well over a century in many parts of the world it was only a decade or so ago that the Game and Wildlife Conservation Trust developed a raft that could be used for both trapping, and detecting the presence of mink.

Basically, the mink raft is a flat-bed float that has a hole cut in the centre of the deck so that a plastic 'tidy basket' fits neatly into it. A rectangular tunnel is placed over this hole to give some protection to the contents of the basket and make the structure look more inviting for inquisitive wildlife.

The dimensions of the tunnel should depend on the size of the live-catch trap you intend to use because when the raft is converted into trapping mode the cage trap should fit snugly inside the housing.

The tidy basket is almost filled to the top with florist's wet oasis foam, and a thin layer of clay is spread onto the top surface. When the raft is floated, water seeps up through the foam and keeps the clay moist and soft. This means that any creature that crosses the clay pad will leave tracks.

This is really where the huge advantage of using rafts for controlling mink comes to the fore. With speculative trapping, any set traps must be visited and checked at least once every day, whether you actually know if there are mink in your area or not. Float a raft with its clay pad prepared, and it monitors what's about. Without a trap in the housing, the raft may only be checked for prints as infrequently as once a week, or even longer.

In its monitoring mode, the raft records anything that has crossed the clay pad and experience will quickly build your practical identification skills. If, one morning, you open the housing and find a mink paw mark on the clay, then it's time to step up a gear.

The clay will often contain the tracks of various species but the mink's pad print is easily recognised.

Now that you know there is a mink about, fit the cage trap into the housing, set the spring door open, and float it back onto the water. You must now visit the raft at least once each day. Remember to take your air rifle with you on each visit, because within a very short while you will find the trap sprung and an aggressive mink within. Having disposed of your first mink, keep the raft in trapping mode for another week or two, and if no others appear, you can return to monitoring – remove the trap, make sure the clay pad is in good order, and revert to weekly or fortnightly visits.

The basic design and construction of the GWCT's pioneering mink raft can be downloaded from their website, and once you get the general idea of how it works, you may wish to adapt it to your own needs by using different materials and fixings. The GWCT design uses a sandwich of expanded foam insulation board between sheets of plywood, and the housing is also a wooden construction. While this produces an immensely strong structure it is very heavy and moving a raft from one site to another requires quite an effort.

BASC and a number of wildlife trusts use a lightweight raft in which the plywood is replaced by corrugated plastic – called Correx in the trade. Cable ties and heavy duty Velcro serve to hold the assembly together, and a tidy basket one size larger than the original design also serves as a stabilising keel when the foam is waterlogged.

Experience has shown that the top deck of the Correx begins to break down from sunlight after two or three years exposure, but the useful life of the raft can be doubled by flipping it over and moving the housing onto the new top surface, so you can expect about five years use from your raft.

Siting your raft

A raft in place on the Somerset Levels.

Provided there is enough water to float the raft, any ditch, stream or pond at least a metre (yard plus) wide will be sufficient to get the raft away from the bank in 'free float'. The mooring rope must be long enough to cope with a rise and fall in the water levels and should be secured to a post in the bank, or to an overhanging tree branch.

Don't forget that the raft isn't exactly streamlined, so on a fast-flowing stream float your raft in the quiet backwaters where a mink is likely to come for a rest.

As well as backwaters and pools, other promising river locations include near a confluence where a side stream enters the main river, near shingle banks on the inside of a bend, and under overhanging trees.

On stillwaters a good choice would be close to the inflow or outflow channels, beside reed beds or close to any other bankside cover. Wherever you choose to float your raft, make sure it is safe from interference by farm animals.

If your ground has no streams or ponds you will have to rely on tunnel trapping. But where a mink raft can be used you will save a lot of time and effort, especially if you use it first to detect mink and only begin trapping when you know that they are around.

8 POISONING

IMAGE BY JEAN MICHEL LABAT/ARDEA.COM

The only pest species that can be legally poisoned and present a threat to game birds and wildlife are rats and grey squirrels.

No one should underestimate the rat as a serious predator. During the warm summer months rats will spread out into crops and hedgerows, and here they can do considerable harm to game and wildlife. A good system of tunnel traps run on the shoot will help to control rats in these situations.

However, in the winter, when the cover is low and food scarce, rats will often congregate in large numbers where there is food and shelter. This concentration gives us a good chance to control their numbers. Do not underestimate their ability to breed and the damage they can do; a few rats left unchecked will multiply rapidly.

There are many methods of controlling rats, and they work best when combined in an overall plan of action. The first thing is to assess the situation; look at the shoot as a whole and then devise an appropriate strategy. It is best to consider all the options before embarking on a rat-poisoning campaign; it should be one of the last choices, not the first.

Start by looking round the farm itself; by keeping things clean and tidy, and putting foodstuffs in containers, you will reduce the places for rats to hide and feed. Putting extra tunnel traps round the buildings will take a fair proportion of rats as they move into the area. Any hoppers on the shoot will attract rats so, again, a tunnel trap sited nearby will be successful.

If, despite your best efforts, rats become established in large numbers, then alternative methods will be needed. They can be shot, bolted with ferrets or taken with terriers at night. They can also be smoked out of their burrows and there are now lightweight smoking machines for this as opposed to the old-fashioned chainsaw with a pipe on the exhaust. The rats are bolted, either to dogs or guns, and this can be entertaining sport as well as providing an alternative to poison.

Gassing can be a good option where there are large infestations of rats, but to do this you should be suitably trained and proficient. Unless you are, leave it to those who are properly qualified.

A combination of all these methods along with poisoning is likely to prove the most

Commercially made box.

successful. If, however, you can control without the need for rodenticides – rat poisons – then so much the better. Remember that poison poses a risk to many other animals and it may be inadvisable to use it because of these risks.

Once you have decided to embark on a programme of poisoning, it is again best to have a planned approach. If you have a large infestation you may decide to employ a professional contractor to deal with the problem; certain types of rodenticides are for trained professionals only; conversely some are for amateur use only.

If you are tackling the problem yourself, ask your supplier which poison suits your needs best because there are different types as well as brands. First-generation products such as warfarin and coumatetralyl carry a significantly reduced risk of secondary poisoning (this is when a scavenger eats a poisoned rodent and in turn becomes poisoned itself) than later second-generation poisons and should be used in preference if you live in an area where rats are not resistant to the first type.

Read the label; you will find what is called the statutory box on it. It is a legal requirement to follow the instructions there, so check that your planned use is compatible with it. Some poisons may only be used indoors. Remember to store it according to the label and always keep it in the original packaging.

Most pre-mixed poisons are grain-based although some will be in pellet or block form, usually with a mould inhibitor (these are still based on grain).

How to use rodenticides

As an example of good practice let's assume that we are using a grain-based product in a hedgerow where gassing is impractical; the fields are too wet and rats to numerous to shoot at night, so we decide that we need to use a rodenticide. We get the poison as advised from our supplier – a first-generation one as we are in an area where rats have not built up immunity. After reading the statutory box and instructions we are ready to go.

In the example described, a good plan would be to site some pipes or purpose-built boxes at regular intervals in the area, all secured so they cannot be moved. These are baited with ordinary wheat which is regularly checked and topped up. Once the rats are confidently feeding from them, swap the untreated wheat for the poisoned wheat and remove any sites that are not being used or have droppings indicating the presence of smaller non-target rodents.

How to make a baiting station using plastic drainpipe

Pipes are cut into lengths of roughly 50cm (20in), with two cuts underneath just over halfway through, about 12cm (4³/₄in) from each end. Then a piece of square metal is tapped in. Drill or cut a large hole in the top, then cover with a sliding piece of pipe.

The metal squares – left slightly longer – are pressed into the ground and, being tight fitting, hold the pipe in place. They also help prevent non-target species accessing the bait.

Use a jug marked with the maximum dose for baiting, and always wear rubber gloves.

The lid can be slid easily to one side with a spade for checking.

Check the poison sites every day and replace the bait that has been removed, but do not be tempted to put more than the correct amount down. Apart from the fact that you may be breaking the law, rats seem to take the wheat – treated

Prevent access to non-target species.

or otherwise – more readily when there is a small amount. Large amounts are often simply hoarded.

Remember to keep a written record of where, when and how much you use. This may sound rather onerous but it will be a way of showing that you have done everything correctly should anything happen; it is also a useful way of gauging how effectively the poison is being used.

While checking and topping up the bait points, also check for any dead rats. Most die in their holes but it is a legal requirement to search for any that may have been poisoned and are accessible to scavengers.

Usually, after a few days, the poisoned wheat stops going and this is a good sign that the job has been done, so then move on to the next area. If you have more than one set of pipes or boxes these can be pre-baited, allowing more intensive control.

Also keep checking the original area for several days to make sure that no rats have died on the surface later. Any bodies that are picked up must be disposed of in accordance with the instructions on the poison container, which generally allow use of the farm's incinerator or deep burial.

By using the poison as described we not only avoid wastage, and so save money, but also minimise the risk of anything else, such as a barn owl, suffering secondary poisoning.

While treating a hedge in this way, do not go lamping in the immediate area for rabbits or rats; it is best to let them feed undisturbed and thus take in sufficient poison to die in the burrow. However, do some lamping a little while after treating the area (picking up and disposing of any rats left in the area) as part of your integrated programme of control.

Always use sufficient baiting points and containers. Commercially made boxes can be bought from poison suppliers but other bait stations can be used. Pipes can be made from lengths of plastic drainpipe, as shown on page 85, and you can also cut a square from an old piece of corrugated tin, roughly 70cm (28in) square, dig a small hole under it and put a square of plastic in it with the bait on top, and this will help stop damp spoiling the poison (pictured left). You can also make bait stations out of other materials such as wooden boxes, but beware of damp and moisture as this can spoil any poison inside.

One of the best methods if the rat holes are easily accessible is to spoon bait directly into them (if the label allows this) and a stout turf, turned grass-side down over the hole, can prevent access by non-target species.

While poisoning is very effective when done properly it can create serious problems if you are less conscientious. If rats eat a non-lethal dose they can become immune to certain types of poison. Don't leave sites with poison just in case a rat comes by – this just increases the risk of secondary poisoning and tunnel traps can deal with them – and do keep checking an active treatment area until no more poison goes.

Finally, rodenticides can be harmful to you and rats themselves can carry some very nasty diseases. Do take precautions; as a minimum wear rubber gloves, do not eat, drink or smoke and always wash your hands afterwards.

Do go on training courses, look at the internet, talk to others and pick up new ideas. We can all learn new techniques and better practices, and just because we have always done it in a particular way does not mean we can't improve.

Remember to plan ahead, you will have more success this way, keep good records and always follow the instructions on the packaging. By sticking to the rules and best practices we will keep a most useful tool for pest control. Recent moves by some European countries regarding a proposed ban on the use of rodenticides highlights the need for everyone to maintain the highest of standards. Every incident of accidental of poisoning of non-target species makes resisting such moves harder.

Squirrels can be controlled with poison under strict regulations, but only for tree protection and only by trained persons. It is therefore outside the scope of this book.

9
GREY SQUIRRELS: trapping and shooting

The grey squirrel is a non-native species which presents a serious threat to habitat and wildlife.

Air rifles can be used effectively – but always go for a head shot.

By stripping bark from saplings they can severely damage trees, resulting in reduced timber value, and in the worst case complete ring-barking will kill trees. They are largely responsible for the extinction of the native red squirrel in most of England and Wales; this is due to their aggressive habits, which drive out the red squirrel, and their role as a carrier of squirrel pox – a disease to which they are largely immune but which is fatal to the reds.

Grey squirrels will readily raid nests for eggs and chicks. This has a serious effect on game birds and has been shown to be a major factor in the decline of songbirds in some areas.

Grey squirrels are not protected and may be dealt with at any time of the year. Shotguns are generally used for squirrel control but the relatively low power of air rifles makes them a good choice when shooting in confined woodland situations.

Autumn through to early spring is the best time to tackle squirrels in the woods. Trying to spot them in thick summer foliage before they spot you and disappear is really difficult and incredibly frustrating.

With a shotgun, opportunist sessions, combined with a stroll through the woods or duties such as trap checking, are the usual options. The noise from a shotgun will alert all the squirrels in a area so you are unlikely to get many shots, though the quick handling will help you to make the most of any opportunities that occur. However it is now possible to buy a moderated .410 which is a very effective tool.

A .22 rimfire or a .17HMR rifle is also effective, especially if moderated, but it is unsafe to use one of these unless the squirrel is on the ground and there is a solid backstop. This inevitably limits your shooting opportunities.

Air rifles are well suited to squirrel control, particularly where the animals are in trees, but remember that accuracy is vital; you should only go for a head shot. When shooting into trees always take account of where the pellets will fall if you miss the target. You have no backstop and a spent pellet can travel for at least 230m (250 yards).

The key to making a real dent in grey squirrel numbers is to identify the areas they like best and target these intensively. Squirrel sightings will reveal the best place to start but, if you don't see any, there are plenty of other signs.

Areas with one or two dreys are well worth staking out, as are any parts of the woodland where exceptionally large, dense patches of ivy provide sheltered habitat. Find a popular food source, such as acorns, beechmast or hazel nuts, in the autumn and action is more or less guaranteed. And don't ignore the attraction of feed hoppers – grey squirrels are suckers for a free meal.

With an air rifle a carefully planned static approach is likely to be particularly productive. Find a suitable spot, settle down quietly and see if anything ventures out. If nothing happens after an hour, move on and try somewhere else. Full camouflage isn't essential for this sort of shooting but it does help and provides extra concealment if a sharp-eyed crow or magpie happens to pitch within range. Remember to keep an eye on the ground because squirrels spend a lot of time foraging on the woodland floor.

When grey squirrels do emerge they can be very fidgety and more than a little tricky to get a steady bead on. The trick is to follow them through the scope until they present a clear, safe head shot. Then, when the shot looks good, click your tongue or purse your lips and make a squeaking noise. This should alarm the squirrel just enough to make it freeze while you compose the shot and pull the trigger.

Squirrels are social animals so it is worth staying put when you bag one – the muzzle blast from a moderated air rifle is barely audible and several squirrels may be taken from the same stand in a short session.

DREY POKING

As most people know, squirrels breed in dreys, which look like huge birds' nests. Often, in fact, they *are* birds' nests – taken over and considerably enlarged. As the name suggests drey poking involves using a long pole to rattle the nest and dislodge the inhabitants so that they can be shot as they flee.

A typical squirrel drey.

Winter is the best time for this, when the dreys are clearly visible and, with the leaf off the trees, it is easy to see the squirrels bolting. And on a cold day the squirrels are more likely to be at home than foraging in the wood.

Poking is essentially a team job – ideally for a team of four, with two working the poles and two covering the tree. In a day a team can clear a lot of dreys in a wood and, as well as shooting the squirrels, destroying the dreys is important. When all the dreys are cleared from a wood in winter it becomes easy to spot new ones made in the summer.

There are a few rules you must adhere to when carrying out this activity. Safety is paramount; Guns should stand well back from the tree and have strict rules about shooting squirrels on the ground.

When using the poles, tap the bottom of the drey gently, this will allow the squirrel to run out slowly and it will probably stop just outside which will give the Guns time to shoot. Never shoot at a squirrel running down a tree; it is better to either let it run down and away from you or stop it and turn it back up the tree. Remember you are aiming to cull squirrels, so be efficient and effective.

Since grey squirrels killed in the winter will often be replaced before the summer, drey poking is only effective as part of a wider control programme, but it can be an important component, nonetheless.

TRAPPING SQUIRRELS

Tunnel traps set for small mammalian predators, described in Chapter 6, will frequently catch squirrels and they can be specifically targeted by placing the trap in an appropriate location. The bases of large trees, and in roots and hollow trees, are particularly effective sites.

The trap's efficiency can be enhanced by using a bait, though this is not necessary if the trap is on a run regularly used by squirrels. Nuts, maize or corn can be used but do remember that these could also attract pheasants so, as always, make sure the trap entrance is well protected.

Live catch traps are also very effective and should always be used where there is a risk of catching red squirrels. There are various types of trap but the principles of their use remain the same.

They are best set beside trees or areas that are known to be used by squirrels or on recognised squirrel runs. Initially the trap should not be set but left baited so that the squirrels gain confidence. Spread a good quantity of bait around the trap and inside it and do this for a few days, gradually decreasing the baited area.

After five days or so, set the trap and only bait inside it. From now on the trap must be visited at least once a day and ideally twice. When an animal is caught it must be humanely dispatched as quickly as possible. As with mink, an air rifle can be used in the trap.

Some people transfer the squirrel from the trap to a sack and, having trapped it in a corner, kill it with a sharp blow to the head. Whatever method you choose be careful – squirrels have a very powerful bite.

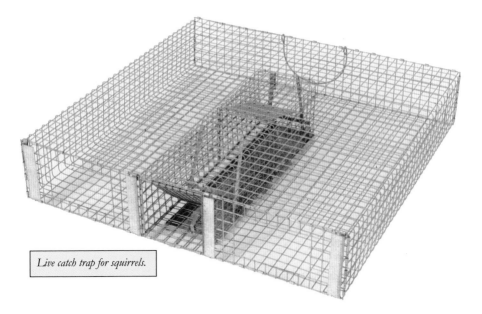

Live catch trap for squirrels.

10 CORVID CONTROL: shooting and trapping

C orvids is the family name by which crows, magpies and their brethren are known. For the modern gamekeeper, trying to protect game and other vulnerable wild birds, corvids can be significant predators of both eggs and chicks. They can also damage farm crops and have a deservedly bad reputation among shepherds for attacking newborn lambs.

Gamekeeper setting wire Larsen trap.

Their numbers have increased significantly in recent years and on conservation grounds there is a clear demand for their control. But modern control is about just that – control: it is management and not eradication.

To begin with, it is important to understand why, and when, game managers need to control these species. There is little point in catching corvids after the breeding season if the sole purpose is protecting gamebird eggs and chicks. However there are often very good reasons, such as preventing damage to crops and livestock, to continue to control crows at other times of the year.

All control of these birds is conducted under the terms of the general licences, explained in Chapter 2. The licences can be found, with explanatory notes, on the relevant authority's Natural England's website and a link to these can be found at www.basc.org.uk

The currently available methods of control are cage trapping and the gun. In order to continue to be allowed to use these methods we must ensure that we do so to the highest of standards.

CORVID SPECIES THAT MAY BE CONTROLLED

ROOK – Adults distinguished from crows by pale base of lower bill and feathery thighs. They have glossy black plumage and are usually found in groups. Immature birds are harder to distinguish from crows as they do not have the pale face.

CARRION CROW – Similar size to rook, adults are territorial in the spring and usually seen alone or in a pair but immature birds and adults outside the nesting season can be found in flocks.

HOODED CROW – Subspecies of the carrion which it replaces in north and west Scotland, Northern Ireland and the Isle of Man. It has grey and black plumage.

MAGPIE – Almost everyone will recognise the magpie; it is virtually unmistakable. The nest is similarly so, in that it is completely enclosed. It is commonly found in thorn bushes and the like.

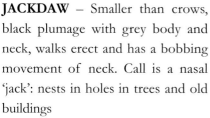

JACKDAW – Smaller than crows, black plumage with grey body and neck, walks erect and has a bobbing movement of neck. Call is a nasal 'jack': nests in holes in trees and old buildings

JAY – Another unmistakable species, winter visitors swell the healthy resident population. Very attractive bird and its winter habit of burying and storing acorns makes it popular with foresters but nonetheless can be a serious egg predator.

LIVE TRAPPING

We have all come to rely on the Larsen trap; for many of us, if we could have only one weapon in the war against winged egg thieves it would be this. Yet the Larsen is a relatively new addition to our arsenal.

They first started to appear in the UK at the end of the 1980s when there was much talk about the burgeoning populations of magpies and crows and the lack of a suitable method of tackling them. The solution came in the form of the Larsen cage which is cost-effective, portable, target-specific – and it works.

In its most simple form it is a cage with a closing door (In Scotland there is a legal definition of one). There is often a compartment for holding a call bird which when placed in the territory of a pair of corvids, provokes them to attempt to drive it away.

Over time new ideas have resulted in many different designs and materials from which Larsens are made. Most will work but everyone has their favourite. Some of the new metal cages painted green can be useful as, from a distance, they are often virtually invisible to the human eye and all that is seen is the call bird. There are square, round, single catch, double and multi catch – the options are numerous.

How does it work?

During the autumn and winter months corvids will often be in flocks, only breaking up in the spring when they then start to pair and take a territory of their own. They defend this fiercely, not tolerating intruders of their own species.

It is this aggression that makes the Larsen work so well. A bird, seeing a rival in its territory, will enter the trap in an attempt to drive it out.

However as soon as one crow or magpie is caught another is often there to take its place, since there will often be a number of unpaired birds on the periphery. If we create a vacuum then they can come in and fill the space, but the trap will continue to take these invaders.

By catching corvids in the spring, disrupting their ability to hold a territory and breed on the shoot, the Larsen is particularly effective. Be careful not to undermine this by setting the trap in the winter. Although the birds will be in flocks then and you may think you are getting ahead of the game, there is a risk that some of the crows will learn to appreciate the danger and become trap-shy, so the job will become much harder in the spring when it really counts. As with all predator control, it is about targeting your resources and time most appropriately.

Larsens will work without a call bird but you have to rely on using food as a bait and the success rate is nowhere near what it is with a call bird. Getting the first bird can be difficult and many people build an aviary to overwinter a call bird or two. If you do this remember that the welfare of these birds (as is also the case with all animals and birds you keep) is your responsibility. Never keep different species in the same pen, as the larger ones will bully the smaller. It is illegal to sell these birds, so if you are acquiring a call bird from another person remember that no payment may be made.

Call birds must be looked after; they should have a shelter, perch, access to clean water and food and must be checked at least once every 24 hours. This is important, as it is not every *day*, as is the case with some other traps. If you check it at 10 o'clock in the morning then it must be checked before 10 o'clock the next morning or you are breaking the law.

When the cage is not in use it must be rendered incapable of catching, so tie the doors with a wire cable and remove the call bird; it is not permitted to leave the call bird in an unset cage.

Larsen trap with magpie as call bird.

For water it is a good idea to use a bottle with a hole cut in the side, which prevent the bird from fouling its water. Another good tip is to use small dried dog food in a container instead of meat. It is easier and cleaner, and it looks more professional should anyone come upon your trap. It is also less likely than meat to attract other scavengers.

If you do catch a non-target species and it is uninjured and healthy just open the door and let it go. It is a good idea to keep a record of all catches and any releases. There are many rumours of keepers being set up; if you do find anything suspicious in or around a cage or trap always call someone who would be a reliable witness and tell them before or immediately after doing anything (another reason for keeping a mobile phone to hand). We do need to be mindful that there are those who would go to extreme lengths to discredit us.

It is also a good idea to have a sign on the cage explaining that it is a legal method of control and that damaging or interfering with it can be a criminal offence. (These are available from BASC's game and gamekeeping department.) There are well-meaning but uneducated people who imagine that any cage is illegal and they are rescuing your call bird. It is often wise, therefore, to try to avoid setting traps where there is a risk of interference.

For magpies side-entry and top-entry traps enjoy a similar success rate, but with crows the side-entry ones tend to work better in early spring when the cover is low. If you set the cage in a more open area, the crows land and tend to walk in.

If you get a particularly suspicious crow there are little tricks that you can try, like putting a side-entry cage on a hedge bank; this raises the call bird a little and stops the crow from walking round the cage. Or you can try raising a top-entry trap on bales or on a frame – this method is especially effective in woodland before the leaf is out on the trees. By raising the cage, the extra height of the call bird triggers the crow's aggression since it does not like the other bird being higher.

As the cover grows, a good tactic for all species is to put a top-entry cage in a situation where only the top is visible. It does not matter that the call bird is not in view; in fact it often works better if it isn't. As the bird calls the only way for the crow to see and to get at it is through the catching compartments.

Each shoot will have places that work best. These may be hedges between woods or near 'sitty trees' (usually a little distance away). Sometimes moving a trap only a few paces, possibly from one side of a hedge to the other, can make the difference between success and failure.

It is best to run the traps continuously through the spring and summer period, only stopping if you are unable to check them. Start them in a few likely-looking places: often the first you see of a magpie or crow is the one in your cage, but if you see a crow or magpie in another area then move a cage there.

If one of a pair is caught, leaving it in the cage a little while longer or swopping it with the call bird can often improve the chances of catching its mate.

Always leave a cage in position for a few days after you have had a catch because a territory has been freed and there may be replacements on the way. Sometimes a call bird will not be working and, if this is the case, replacing it with another can give better results. It is also a good idea to rotate call birds.

Crows – carrion and hooded – are very clever and do seem to be harder to catch than other corvids, but by working the cages and being prepared to move them regularly and experiment success is achievable.

LARGER CAGE TRAPS

Larsen cages are great when you are dealing with pairs of birds and need to be flexible and mobile. However there may be times when you have large flocks of crows, rooks and jackdaws that need controlling.

Rubbish dumps or places such as outdoor pig units where food is thrown to livestock can attract and sustain unnaturally high numbers of corvids. Come the spring these will make serious inroads into any wild bird's eggs in the area.

One of the most effective methods of control is the large cage trap. These come in a variety of designs and can be permanent or semi-portable.

Another design which is popular for jackdaws is the letterbox or ladder trap. This can take a little more carpentry skill. As you see from the picture below the sides slope down to a ladder. The rungs are roughly 15cm (6in) in length by 23cm (9in) apart. They do not run to the ends of the cage; this is filled in by wire.

Jackdaws are clever birds and can climb up the wire sides and back out, so it is also a good idea to put a wire skirt of 15cm (6in) round the ladder opening to prevent escape. When making cages of this type, weathered timber is best as it blends in quickly with the surroundings. A good tip with this design is to make the cage fit inside a suitably sized farm trailer, if you have access to one.

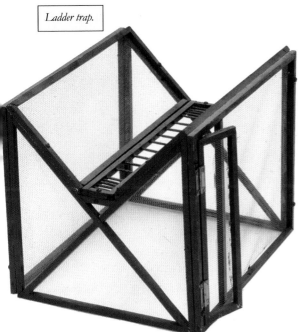

Ladder trap.

Remember to give any captive or call birds the same care as in the Larsen; they need shelter, perches, clean food and water, and make sure there is sufficient for any extra birds you may catch. These cages can also be a good place to overwinter call birds: many keepers will retain several of the caught birds to act as decoys for the coming days.

Since they are obviously less portable and more visible than

Larsens, some thought must be given to siting large cage traps. This has a huge effect on how well they catch. A little time spent on reconnaissance identifying favoured areas can pay off, but never been afraid to move a cage which is not working well. Often they can be built where a Larsen has proved continually successful, or where there is an established food source, but do try to keep them away from public view.

When using them to catch large numbers of corvids, often jackdaws and rooks around the sites mentioned earlier, it is necessary to have them in place and prebaited for a while before you close the trap. Remove the roof so the birds are used to going inside. A good tip, if you are using a letterbox, is to leave the ladder in place, but remove the top sides so that they get used to sitting on and dropping through the rungs. The birds then become accustomed to entering and feeding without suspicion.

Finally, always use an appropriate bait. To use the pig unit mentioned above as an example, food pellets that the crows are used to feeding off, scattered around the pen, are the natural choice. Other good baits can be dead rabbits or bread.

Dispatching caught birds

Crows in particular can have quite a nasty peck, capable of drawing blood, so a thick glove is often a good precaution. Remove the bird from the cage, hold the wings tight to the body and break its neck, either with a pair of purpose-made dispatching pliers or, if competent, this can be done very swiftly by pushing the head forward and upwards at the same time. Failing this, a swift blow with a priest is recommended.

If you are dispatching large numbers in a cage, using a hessian sack to hold and dispatch the bird out of sight causes less alarm to the others. Remember that any commotion in the pen can alert a wary bird on the outside to the dangers. Always dispose of any that you dispatch appropriately.

Control of corvids is an essential part of protecting game and wildlife but it should be part of an overall plan. At times of the year when these birds do not present a serious problem the time spent on their control might be better spent elsewhere.

HOW TO BUILD A CAGE TRAP

To build a cage trap you will need:

- 24 x 1.8–2m (6ft–6ft 6in) lengths of 47mm x 50mm (1⅞in x 2in) sawn timber
- 25m (27 yards) wire netting
- wire staples
- 100mm (4in) screws or nails, plus smaller screws for pen section corners
- sheet plywood
- bolt and hinges for the door, 10 x 10cm (4in) coach bolts (optional)

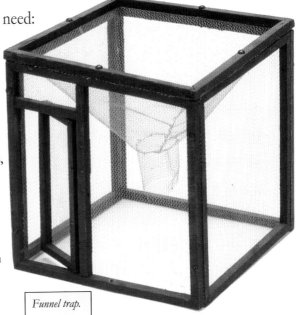

Funnel trap.

The ideal size for a cage trap is 3m (length) by 2m x 2m (9ft 9in x 6ft 6in x 6ft 6in). Each side is made like a pheasant pen section, with triangles of ply in each corner for bracing. A simple hinge door is incorporated on one of the sides and the funnel is made from four pieces of netting suspended from the roof section. Remember, when buying your timber, that the roof will have to be a little bit larger than each of the sides, so some lengths need to be slightly longer for the roof.

The funnel should be 1m (3ft 3in) square at the top, tapering to 60cm (2ft) in diameter at the base, and the base should sit about 23–25cm (9–10in) off the ground.

Depending on your skills, it takes about a day to make the trap and all the components are readily available at any do-it-yourself or hardware shop.

A permanent trap could be nailed or screwed together in situ, but if you want to move it around it can be bolted together with ten 10cm (4in) coach bolts.

SHOOTING CORVIDS

The keeper, whether full-time or amateur, will often account for quite a head of pests by carrying his gun with him on his daily rounds. It is, however, a classic example of Murphy's law that if you are carrying a shotgun the crow will immediately sit out of range in a field while, if you are carrying a rifle, it will flit overhead.

As with most species, crows tend to congregate where there is food and this is often the best place to control them. A newly drilled crop or wind-blown barley can be hit hard by corvids and it is best to deal with these as you would with pigeons – by decoying and using a shotgun.

The basics are the same; a good hide and plenty of camouflage with decoys in position. Some people do very well with a couple of rooks on a rotary device but this is not always effective and a couple placed on floaters, gently swaying in the breeze, usually works well.

Any birds that are shot can be set up to bolster the pattern and it's important to place them in a lifelike position because birds on their backs or in unnatural positions have exactly the opposite effect and scare off incomers. Within reason the more decoys you can put out, the better. It's often effective to put out pigeon decoys initially, replacing them with shot birds as they arrive.

To protect gamebirds' eggs and chicks in the spring a similar plan can be employed. An early morning ambush with a lure such as a stuffed fox or plastic owl decoy may produce good results, but it is important to be out before the crows; they won't come in if they know you are there, and good camouflage is essential.

Calls can be effective but remember that tethered decoys and sound recordings are not allowed. As well as shotguns, rifles can also be effective. If you can bring the birds in close, a moderated air rifle can be used provided you are capable of killing cleanly with a head shot. Otherwise a rifle that has been approved by the police can be used, which allows longer-range shots, provided there is an effective backstop.

These methods rely on you attracting the bird to you; the alternative is to know where the crows will be and ambush them there. This could involve waiting on a flight line or staking out the crow's nest.

In early spring, well before the leaf starts to come out, patrol your ground and note where the nests of crows and magpies are; some people shoot the old ones out so that they can tell the new active ones. Whether you do that or not, it's important to spot them early because once the trees are in leaf the nests can be impossible to find.

Despite the use of cage traps and Larsens, even the best of keepers can have a crow or magpie nesting on their ground, and once established they can become immune to trapping, so knowing where the nest site is can give you a chance.

Two methods can work; the first is to sneak up to the tree and shout to put the bird off the nest. It will slip away very quickly and be a testing target, so if you are not a good shot take someone who is.

The other method, which works well when the bird sees your approach and leaves the nest before you arrive, is to take a companion; one leaves while the other stays. It is imperative to be well hidden, with face and hands camouflaged, and to stay absolutely still until the shot is taken.

These nesting birds are exceptionally wary, so it is best to try this tactic on a cool evening. Then it is usually only a matter of minutes before the bird returns, whereas during the warmth of the day they will stay away for quite some time. Once the adult has been dispatched be certain not to leave eggs or, more importantly, chicks in the nest. A few well-placed shots using suitably sized cartridges will penetrate and destroy them.

Jays tend to nest later than other corvids so their nests are often more difficult to find. They are seldom elaborate structures – often no more than a platform of twigs.

Rooks' nests are very similar in appearance to crows' nests but they are gregarious birds, nesting communally in large rookeries.

Jackdaws nest in old buildings and hollows of trees.

Other corvids can be controlled in a similar manner. However, old disused nests may be occupied by other birds; nest sites suitable for jackdaws are also favourites with owls and other species, so make sure you are absolutely certain that you have correctly identified the occupant.

The magpie's nest is pretty much unmistakable; the canopy of twigs above the base gives the appearance of a lid.

Crows are solitary nesters and the location can vary from the middle of a wood to a lone tree with a good lookout.

All corvid control, like all wildlife management, should be sustainable and balanced. There will be times when these birds can be beneficial. As an example, jays are well known for burying acorns, some of which will be left and will grow into oak trees. The potential for good should therefore be weighed against the harm inflicted and control must be proportionate to the species and the circumstance.

11 NON-LETHAL METHODS OF CONTROL

In release pens avoid sharp corners.

While much pest control relies on killing target species there are occasions when this is not feasible. The obvious case is where a predator is protected by law but there may be situations where consideration for other wildlife or neighbours precludes lethal methods. Or you may simply not have the opportunity to check snares and traps as frequently as is necessary.

A well-sited electric fence.

With the general licences, under which much lethal control is carried out, there is often a reference to considering non-lethal methods first. These licences tell you that they can only be relied on in circumstances where the person who is using the licence is satisfied that 'appropriate legal methods of resolving the problem such as scaring and proofing are either ineffective or impracticable'.

In practice this does not mean that you must have actually tried the methods. There is no need to produce a written assessment or provide concrete evidence that non-lethal methods have been tried and failed. It is really just a case of being certain in your own mind.

Control of predators actually starts long before we ever set a trap, snare or fire a shot; almost without realising it, non-lethal deterrence will be part of our initial planning. It's a consideration in how we plan and build a release pen, how we manage released birds' welfare and how they will spread out after release.

In the pen we avoid tight corners and provide plenty of cover as well as fortifying it with traps and electric fences, and site it well away from badger setts or regular nesting sites for birds of prey. Outside the pen avoid long, straight feed rides. Curving rides with plenty of nearby cover for the birds to hide in make it more difficult for raptors to strike. Some shoots, when releasing small numbers, will use a covered pen to give added protection.

Once the birds arrive we can deploy a variety of methods; flashing lights such as those used on roadworks, an old coat or scarecrow hung on the fence, empty feedbags hung from trees to blow in the wind or CDs that catch the light can all help, and a radio tuned to a station with a lot of talking is a good idea.

Probably the most common form of non-lethal protection is an electric fence – one strand or sometimes two round the perimeter of the pen. Make sure it is working well before any birds arrive: there are special meters to measure this if you do not have an unsuspecting syndicate member to test it on! It must be far enough from the pen to deter digging under the wire but close enough to prevent a fox from jumping over. It must also be clear from vegetation for the whole of its length and correctly earthed to prevent it shorting out.

The key to successful deterrence, except by physical barriers, is to prevent familiarity, which in this case really does breed contempt. Where possible try to vary your methods and remember that some could backfire. Leaving hedges and hedge banks uncut provides both food and cover for birds to hide from predators; this is obviously beneficial but it can also provide cover for stoats and weasels, and more cover may demand more trapping.

On the subject of cover, when planting game crops many shoots will factor in their ability to provide shelter from winged predators when making their choice.

So deterrence, like everything else, should be part of an overall strategy. There really is not a one-size-fits-all solution. A mixture of all the methods of control available and the correct way of combining them, at the appropriate time, whether they are lethal or not, will give the best results.

THE TERRIER CODE OF PRACTICE

Introduction

1. The Code of Practice set out below has the force of law. It sets out the manner in which a dog may be legally used below ground in the course of stalking or flushing out a wild mammal in accordance with paragraph 2 of Schedule 1 to the Hunting Act 2004 (so long as the other conditions in the exemption are also met).

2. Failure to comply with the conditions of the exemption or with the Code set out below will mean that the use of a dog below ground to hunt wild mammals is no longer exempt hunting and will therefore be a criminal offence which may result in prosecution and a fine of up to £5,000. Failure to observe this Code may also lead to disciplinary action by organisations endorsing this code, and this may result in expulsion, consequential loss of shooting insurance and professional opportunity.

3. The Code of Practice is supported by a Good Practice Guide. While not having the force of law, this Guide covers a range of activities which are compatible with the Act and this Code, and compliance with the Good Practice Guide might be relevant to whether activity has been undertaken in accordance with the Code.

4. Although the commonly used terms 'terrier' and 'terrier work' are used in this Code they should be understood as referring to any type of dog and to any use of a dog below ground.

5. All relevant animal welfare and other legislation must be observed by anyone intending to rely on this Code and the exemption. By law, only one terrier can be used in an earth at any one time.

The Code

6. The following principles must always be observed when a terrier is used below ground to stalk or flush out a wild mammal:

> The terrier's role must be to locate the wild mammal underground and cause it to 'bolt' (leave the earth or den) as soon as possible so that it can be shot by a competent person and humanely dispatched. It should not be intended that a terrier will fight the wild mammal.

> Only terriers that are 'soft' (those that habitually stand off and bark at the wild mammal) must be used. Terriers that are 'hard' (those that habitually fight) must not be used.

> Care must always be taken to ensure the safety of those involved and to minimise the risk of injury to either the wild mammal or terrier during the bolting process.

> The terrier's time underground should be kept as short as possible so as to minimise any potential distress to the wild mammal.

The terrier being used must always be fitted with an electronic locator so that its exact position underground can be tracked.

Once it is determined that a terrier has become trapped assistance must be given to release it.

Approved for the purpose of paragraph 2 of Schedule 1 to the Hunting Act 2004 by the Secretary of State for Environment, Food and Rural Affairs on the 17th February 2005.

APPENDIX II

FURTHER READING AND CONTACTS

Further reading

Animal Tracks and Signs by Preben Bang and Preben Dahlstrom. Oxford University Press ISBN 978-0-19-929997-3

Fair Game – the Law of Country Sports by Charlie Parkes and John Thornley. Pelham Books ISBN 07207 20656

Foxing with Lamp and Rifle by Robert Bucknell. Foxearth Publishing ISBN 978-0-9540206-1-3

Gamekeeping by David Hudson. Quiller ISBN 978-1-904057-73-4

Hunting with Air Rifles: the Complete Guide by Mathew Manning. Northumbria Press ISBN 978-0-85716-001-0

The BASC Handbook of Shooting. Quiller ISBN 978-1-84689-059-8

The Deer Stalking Handbook by Graham Downing. Quiller ISBN 978-1-84689-048-2

The Pigeon Shooter by John Batley. Quiller ISBN 978-1-904057-51-2

The Sporting Rifle: a User's Handbook by Robin Marshall-Ball. Quiller ISBN 978-1-84689-055-0

BASC codes of practice

Lamping (night shooting)
Terriers
Airguns
These, and codes covering other aspects of shooting, can be downloaded from the BASC website. Hard copies are available on request.

Contacts

Remember that the law and the regulations covering pest and predator control are liable to change and it is easy to be caught out. The following organisations and websites will generally be able to keep you up to date.

British Association for Shooting and Conservation
Marford Mill
Rossett
Wrexham LL12 0HL
Tel: 01244 573000
Email enq@basc.org.uk
Website www.basc.org.uk

BASC Scotland Centre
Trochry
Dunkeld
Tayside PH8 0DY
Tel: 01350 723226
Email scotland@basc.org.uk

BASC Wales Centre
The Station House
Caersws
Powys SY17 5HH
Tel: 01686 688 861
Email wales@basc.org.uk

BASC Northern Ireland Centre
33 Castle Street
Lisburn
Co Down BT27 4SP
Tel: 028 9260 5050
Email nire@basc.org.uk

BASC's specialist departments give free advice to members:

BASC game and gamekeeping department
01244 573019
gamekeeping@basc.org.uk

BASC firearms department
01244 573010
firearms@basc.org.uk

For details of BASC membership visit www.basc.org.uk or call 01244 573030

Natural England
0845 600 3078
enquiries@naturalengland.org.uk
for wildlife licensing enquiries
0845 6014523
wildlife@naturalengland.org.uk

Think Wildlife – the Campaign for Responsible Rodenticide Use
www.thinkwildlife.org.uk

Game and Wildlife Conservation Trust
01425 652381
info@gwct.org.uk
www.gwct.org.uk

Spring Trap Approval Orders
For England, Wales and Northern Ireland
www.legislation.gov.uk and search 'spring traps approval order'
For Scotland
www.scotland.gov.uk/Resource/Doc/1221/0050637.pdf

INDEX